Tetum
Ghosts & Kin

D1059388

SECOND EDITION

Tetum
Ghosts & Kin

FERTILITY AND GENDER IN EAST TIMOR

DAVID HICKS
Stony Brook University

WAVELAND
PRESS, INC.

Long Grove, Illinois

**To my wife,
Maxine**

For information about this book, contact:
Waveland Press, Inc.
4180 IL Route 83, Suite 101
Long Grove, IL 60047-9580
(847) 634-0081
info@waveland.com
www.waveland.com

10-digit ISBN 1-57766-265-2
13-digit ISBN 978-1-57766-265-5

Printed in the United States of America

8   7   6   5   4   3

Contents

Preface to the First Edition

Anthropology, like all scientific and artistic disciplines, is constantly changing so that research approaches once generally favored inevitably give way to new approaches over time. One of the most important developments in cultural anthropology has been the attempt to analyze cultural phenomena in terms of their symbolic significance instead of, or in addition to, their structural, functional, and ecological significance, an approach that is often referred to as symbolic anthropology.

Religion, of course, is the primary arena for symbolic meanings and acts. Therefore it is not at all surprising that the advent of symbolic anthropology has been accompanied by a resurgence of interest in the study of non-Western, nonliterate religions. This revival has been particularly marked in British social anthropology, of which Professor Hicks is representative. By concentrating on ghosts and kin in this analysis of the symbols employed in the rituals of Tetum society, Professor Hicks enables us to understand much of how the social lives of the Tetum people relate to their rituals and collective ideas. Thus the book is not only a useful example of symbolic analysis, but it also demonstrates the functional integration of culture, which has fascinated anthropologists for at least the past half century.

Robert B. Edgerton
L. L. Langness

vii

Preface to the Second Edition

This is a study of rituals of reproduction and regeneration in a society located in East Timor, a country in the region that used to be known as the East Indies, which obtained its independence on 20 May 2002. It shows how rituals of fertility dominate the ritual life of the Tetum-speaking peoples of the *suku* of Caraubalo, in the district of Viqueque. It also describes the implications for Tetum life that the source of fertility, tapped by ritual for the benefit of humanity, is considered to lie in the world of the dead.

In July 1999, while waiting in the airport at Dili, East Timor's capital, to board my flight to Bali, I was approached by a young man who looked like a student. We started chatting, and during the course of our conversation we happened to exchange names. When he heard mine he asked if I was the author of a book on East Timor, and I admitted that such was indeed the case, since an Indonesian translation of *Tetum Ghosts and Kin* had appeared from the Penerbit Sinar Harapan publishing house in Jakarta 14 years previously. He then told me that the book was assigned reading in his school in Suai, a district located on the southern coast of East Timor.

The notion of writing a second edition of *Tetum Ghosts and Kin* had occurred to me over the years. When it appeared in 1976 it was the first ethnography to have been published by a professional social anthropologist on East Timor, but in the intervening years since its publication several other books and a number of doctoral dissertations have since

ix

greatly expanded our knowledge of the peoples of this region. Furthermore, more than 30 years of teaching social anthropology had caused me to see more possibilities in the ethnographic information I had collected and thus to rethink certain of my ideas regarding how best to conceptualize my interpretation of Tetum society as I understood it to be in the 1960s. It was, however, the realization that Timorese people themselves evidently found some interest in what I wrote about one of their communities that put my idea of writing a second edition, which I had earlier shared with my editor at Waveland Press, Jeni Ogilvie, into action. This decision was strengthened by two further visits I subsequently made to East Timor, one of which was to Caraubalo *suku*, in the district of Viqueque, where—as readers of the first edition will know—I had carried out most of my earlier fieldwork.

This return visit to Caraubalo lasted mere days, but the alterations—and obliterations—I saw in the people's lives convinced me to flesh out in more detail the ethnographic particularities of Caraubalo as it was in the 1960s, and amplify what I wrote in the original edition about gender in a Timorese community. The ethnographic information from which this argument derives is for the most part based on the results of my first period in the field, but I have incorporated some new information that has since come my way. In this edition, accordingly, I intend on occasion to indulge a privileged hindsight when it serves my intention of presenting a clearer picture of how the people of Caraubalo lived before the despoliation wrought over the course of almost a quarter of a century by the Indonesian government. The portrait is intended to describe how life in a Viqueque *suku* was lived in the last years of one of the oldest European colonies of the twentieth century.

In the first edition of *Tetum Ghosts and Kin* I put forward the case that Tetum society in the *suku* of Caraubalo could be interpreted in terms of complementary dualism and a pair of leitmotifs, which might be characterized as "union leading to creation" and "separation leading to re-creation." This demonstration I expanded on with greater detail in a second book on the Tetum, *A Maternal Religion: The Role of Women in Tetum Myth and Ritual*, which was published in 1984. It examined the way rituals were performed; analyzed the contents of myths, legends, and folktales; and considered the semantics of certain symbolically charged words and phrases. In contrast to *A Maternal Religion*, which offers an uncompromisingly structural approach to ritual and belief, *Tetum Ghosts and Kin* focuses on an issue that the comparative ethnographic literature of the East Indies suggests is of widespread importance in the ritual lives of many ethnic groups of the region. I am talking about fertility and life, and the influence the spirit world is credited with having on these essential elements of human life. More specifically, I am interested in Tetum notions concerning the role the ancestors play in promoting fertility and ensuring life. Notions of gender come into play, too, and I shall demonstrate how male and female fertility are regarded as making decidedly different contributions to human existence. I have also incorporated information on cockfighting and kickfighting, which I obtained from all four visits to East Timor, and have made some corrections to certain ethnographic points of detail. In completely reworking the substance of its predecessor I have also taken advantage, in this new edition, of the work of the geographer, Joachim Metzner, who carried out research in Viqueque soon after I had left. His masterly study of this region is indispensable for anyone wanting to know the ecological context in which Timorese institutions function.

The word "Tetum" may be pronounced with or without a nasalized termination, and can be written as Tetun (or Tettun) or Tetu (or Teto). Portuguese orthography avoids a terminal *n* for words, and so in Portuguese writing the spelling Tetu*m* is used. Since my fieldwork was carried out during the time East Timor was subject to Portugal's governance I followed the Portuguese rather than the Dutch orthography, which uses the *n,* and since this usage appears to have won favor with the new political leaders of East Timor there is all the more reason to use it. At various times in this book I refer to the unit of currency used in East Timor during the period 1966 to 1970. On June 26, 1969 the rate of exchange about 3.50 U.S. cents to an *escudo.* The translations of the various categories of oral literature that appear in this book are essentially my own. For the most part I provide free translations from the Tetum original rather than literal translations, but I hope at some time to provide the original Tetum text and subject each to a detailed analysis. I collected all my own texts in the Tetum language in Caraubalo, and the individuals who were generous enough to provide them (and in many cases to help me translate) I note as a group in the acknowledgements.

Acknowledgments

I wish to thank the villagers of Viqueque district without whose help my field research would have been impossible, and the following individuals and institutions for their assistance: Professor Sir Edward Evan Evans-Pritchard, Professor Christoph von Fürer-Haimendorf, Dr. Ravi Jain, Professor H. G. Schulte Nordholt, Dr. Barbara Ward, Mr. Rui Cinatti, Dr. José Teles, Mr. John Burton, the Junta de Investigações do Ultramar, and the Frederick Soddy Trust. My fieldwork was made possible by a grant from the London Committee of the London-Cornell Project for East and Southeast Asian Studies, which was supported jointly by the Carnegie Corporation of New York and the Nuffield Foundation.

Before leaving for Timor I had the advantage of studying social anthropology at Oxford University in the scholarly havens provided by St. Edmund Hall in my first year and Exeter College in subsequent years. To the Principal and Fellows of St. Edmund Hall and to the Rector and Fellows of Exeter College go my profound thanks. I am especially grateful for the honor the Rector and Exeter Fellows bestowed on me by my election to the Alan Coltart Scholarship in Anthropology in 1963–1964 and again in 1964–1965.

Much of the material examined in the book was analyzed while I was a doctorate student at Oxford working under the supervision of Dr. Rodney Needham. My personal and scholarly debt to him is incalculable. Dr. Melody Trott, of California State College, commented on an earlier version of the present text, as did Drs. Robert Edgerton and Lew Langness of the University of California, and my colleague at the State University of New York at Stony Brook, Dr. W. Arens. With extraordinarily painstaking care Mr. Gene Tanke went over my entire manuscript and helped improve it in many ways. Mrs. Mari Walker typed and retyped various drafts in her usual patient manner, and I thank her yet again.

Many of my descriptions of Tetum life were first presented to my own freshmen and graduate students at Stony Brook, and their reactions helped shape the account given here. I completed the first edition of this book while a Fellow of the École Pratique des Hautes Études (University of Paris) in 1976, and I wish to thank the SSRC Fellowship Panel in the U.K. and the EPHE in Paris for providing me with the opportunity to exchange ethnographic information and discuss the interpretation of data with those of my French colleagues who have also carried out fieldwork on Timor—Drs. Brigitte Clamagirand, Claudine Berthe, and Gérard Francillon. Their contributions to the seminar series I gave from February to May helped me to regard my Tetum ethnography from alternative points of view, and it was an agreeable experience working with them. Drs. Pierre Smith and Dan Sperber provided me with sounding boards for certain of my ideas, and they, too, merit my thanks.

It gives me special pleasure to remark on the encouragement that Gabor Nadasty, Marietta Nadasty, Phyllis Newman, Jack and Nancy Garraway, and my mother, Anastasia Dorothy Hicks, gave me at different times while I was writing this book; and as an affectionate token of appreciation for the help she has selflessly given—and continues to give—I rededicate it to my wife, Maxine.

Since writing the first edition, I had the considerable pleasure of visiting Timor a further three times. I therefore reaffirm my gratitude to the people of Viqueque, especially my friends in the Costa Soares family, such as Luís da Costa Soares, Rosa Maria da Costa Soares, and Maria Rosa Biddlecombe, who have grown more cherished to my wife and me with the passing of the years. In the pages that follow I make use of a number of narratives and ritual speeches that various individuals gave me on different occasions. Among these persons were José Pereira, Agostinha, David Soares, João Lopes, and Edmundo. Mr. Constâncio Pinto and Mrs. Gabriella Pinto helped me with interpreting the text on Friarbird that João Lopes and Edmundo had recited for me.

For encouraging me to write this second edition I thank Jeni Ogilvie, my editor at Waveland. The American Philosophical Society awarded me a grant with which to carry out research in East Timor in 1999 and the present edition of *Tetum Ghosts and Kin* has benefited substantially from the Society's generous assistance. A residency at the Rockefeller Foundation's Bellagio Center in Italy enabled me to work on the manuscript free from all academic distractions, and I wish to express my appreciation for the Foundation making this possible. Stony Brook University granted me a sabbatical that enabled me to take advantage of this opportunity.

Chapter 1

Introduction

For the Tetum-speaking peoples of East Timor death and life are conceived of as being located in the same source. This source is the world of the spirit, and for human beings its most immediate manifestation is a class of beings the Tetum refer to as *mate bein*, "ghosts of the ancestors" or "ghosts." Death comes from a variety of sources in this sacred world, and agencies of death include nature spirits, dead souls, and the ghosts. But from these elementals also derive fertility and the gift of life.

Ancestors engage their human kin in the quest for life by their authority to confer or withhold fertility. In this relationship, life force is perpetuated from earlier generations to the as yet unrealized generation of potential kin. These future generations receive it via the agency of the current generation of men and woman who engage themselves in the biological acts and perform the rituals required for its transmission.

Fertility and Life

In discussing the significance of ritual, Arthur Maurice Hocart (1954:19) has written that rituals "have as their purpose to produce or increase the necessaries of life. They are acts of creation. They create more witchetty grubs, more buffaloes, more clouds, or whatever the desired objects may be. The cosmic rites create more of everything that man may need, and as the food supply depends on the proper working of the whole world, such ceremonies create the world." If we discount a certain degree of hyperbole—since ritual intends more than Hocart acknowl-

1

edged—this robust affirmation does draw attention to the connection
between ritual and the human need to find sustenance and reproduce, a
link that one might suppose would be especially marked among populations living in conditions of marginal security brought about by precarious natural factors or by a lack of technological knowledge. By
demonstrating this association among a community of Tetum-speaking
peoples for whom infertility and death are the adversaries of humankind,
I shall demonstrate how the spiritual (or sacred) is the source of fecundity
and how the land itself operates as an interface between the spiritual and
the material,[1] a zone where humanity and the spiritual agencies pool, as
it were, their resources in a manner consistent with Hocart's plangent
affirmation. It argues that the majority of public rituals performed by the
Tetum have as their main purpose the reproduction of life, be it human,
animal, or plant, and demonstrates that so predominating in the ritual
system are these imperatives that they encompass even the death ritual,
which is made into a primary vehicle for replicating life.

The position of women in the ritual systems of the East Indies has
received surprisingly little attention considering this region of Southeast
Asia is one in which connotations of femininity have long been shown to
be of notable ideological importance, as Gregory Forth (1981:206) reaffirms for the Rindi of Sumba, among whom the dead (regardless of their
gender) are said to be symbolically feminine. In Viqueque, for those seek-
ing life, in both a pragmatic sense and a ritual sense, femininity, inflected
sometimes in the form of married women *(feto uma kain)* and sometimes
in the form of unmarried girls *(fetora)* or virgins *(lalosan)* (Hull 1999:193) is
central to the generation of life. The association the Tetum-speaking people make between femininity and the sacred in their religion inclines
towards assigning the female gender a conjunctive role in life, one in
which nurturing is fundamental. The female gender is treated as though it
brings fertile entities together. Men, on the other hand, are inclined
towards ritual roles that lend themselves to disjunctive purposes, as in
separating the dead from the living, as occurs in the death ritual (chapter
6). This gender contrast is given more complexity by the identification of
men with secular *(saun)* concerns, as in political authority, rather than
with sacred or spiritual *(lulik)* matters.

Women, in particular, mediate between human beings and spirits, a
relationship that reproduces and nurtures life as it contributes to the
indigenous definition of womanhood *(feto)*. They do this by means of ritual sacrifice. Palm wine, betel and areca, betel juice, blood, buffaloes,
pigs, and chickens are offered in sacrifice principally by women to various
categories of spirits, an emphasis on the female sex all of a piece with the
natural fertility of women, whose contact with the spiritual is thereby
enhanced. Women's capacity for reproduction is most institutionally

manifested in marriage, the fertilizing character of which affords a symbolic analogy for agricultural rituals.

In part, these rituals are devices for accessing the fertilizing authority of the spirit. Since masculinity is thought to be more closely associated with the secular world and femininity with the spiritual world, the relationship between the sexes can be regarded as corresponding, in ritual contexts, to one between the material world and the spiritual world. This gendered contrast between matter and spirit receives recognition in the conjunctive authority of ritual as it summons up fertility from the domain of death.

References to fertility and life are common enough in the literature of the eastern archipelago. To cite only three instances: R. H. Barnes (1974:104, 105, 109) reports the connection the Kédang of Lomblen make between fertility, life, wealth, and the ground. Gregory Forth (1998:246), from Flores, in discussing the attributes of Nage ancestors writes that "In return for offerings of cooked food, ancestral spirits provide fertility and the means of life and welfare." Finally, Andrea Molnar (2000:208) in informing us of the explanation given by the Hoga Sara of Flores for infertility remarks on the ancestors' "life-generating potential" and how its withdrawal from human beings results in "deaths and discontinuity." The motif of fertility as a force in the ritual lives of the inhabitants in a range of societies throughout this ethnographic region is thus well-attested to and it will be seen that in the symbolic associations attending their concept of life the population discussed in this monograph are typical enough of the region. Their principal interest lies in the consistent emphasis that life and fertility have in their rituals, and I shall try to show how pervasive these ideas are in their culture. In other regions far removed from the confines of insular Southeast Asia, it might be remarked, notions of fertility and life can also figure decisively in the symbolic classification of local societies, as Carol Delaney (1991) has demonstrated for rural community life in Turkey. Hence one purpose of the present investigation into Tetum ritual and collective representations is to add to our understanding of reproductive rituals in a wider comparative sense.

The society I discuss here is a community formed by the population of the two villages, Mamulak and Mane Hat, which together make up the aristocratic half of a princedom known as Caraubalo. This princedom is found in one of the three main regions inhabited by the Tetum people of eastern Indonesia. Certain details of culture and society in Mamulak differ from those in Mane Hat, and I shall point these out when such divergences are important, but otherwise, when making observations common to both villages I shall use the names Mamulak and Mane Hat indiscriminately.

To put this first chapter in its proper context, here is a sketch of the book as a whole. I begin by summarizing my main themes, providing a synopsis of Timorese history, and discussing the circumstances of my fieldwork (chapter 1). Then I consider certain concepts, fundamental to Tetum ritual behavior (chapter 2). In chapter 3 I examine the importance of land in relation to ideas regarding spirits and fertility. Chapter 4 examines the household, lineage, and clan in their socially reproductive capacities. Chapter 5 extends the theme of fertility and gender by considering the social implications of marriage. In chapter 6 I describe the regeneration of the dead as ancestral forces for life and assess the significance of the ghosts in Caraubalo Tetum society. Finally, in chapter 7 I look back on what has happened to the people of Timor since my initial field research in 1966–1967.

East Timor in the Historical Past

Among our earliest sources for the pre-European history of Timor (figure 1) are Chinese documents that identify Timor as "Ti-wu," and by the seventh century A.D. the island had come to be regarded as a source of the finest quality white sandalwood, which seems to have been traded to western Indonesia and perhaps to India as early as A.D. 100 or A.D. 200 (Wolters 1967:65). The Portuguese writer, Tomé Pires, remarks that even before Portuguese sailors reached Timor, Indian merchants were visiting eastern Indonesia for sandalwood, wax, and spices (Cortesão 1944:46). Towards the end of the twelfth century A.D. the island may have been a dependency of a Javanese kingdom, and by the fourteenth century a dependency of the Javanese empire of Majapahit (Coèdes 1968).

The earliest Europeans to glimpse Timor were almost certainly Portuguese sailors sometime between 1500 and 1514, and after that it appears that they visited the island pretty much on an annual basis. The initial attraction was the sandalwood, but in 1556, on a northern coastal site called Lifau, in what was later to become the district of Oé-Cussi, a cleric, Friar António Taveira, began a Dominican quest for converts. His enterprise seems to have flourished since thousands of pagan natives reportedly were converted (Matos 1974:41). The people of Samoro, a settlement in a Tetum-speaking region to the west of Viqueque, mythologized this initial encounter between themselves and Friar António Taveira (Sá 1961:104–13) in the following terms.

> One day, according to the myth, when many kings, their warriors, and all the indigenous priests gathered in the house of the queen of Lifau to conduct a big ritual, they suddenly saw a ship appear on the sea and approach their shores. The queen sent emissaries to the beach. As the

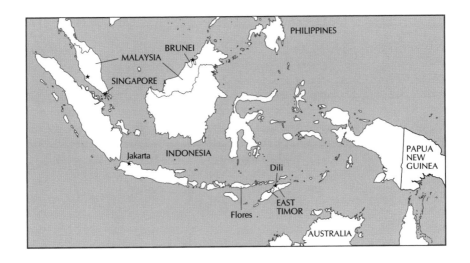

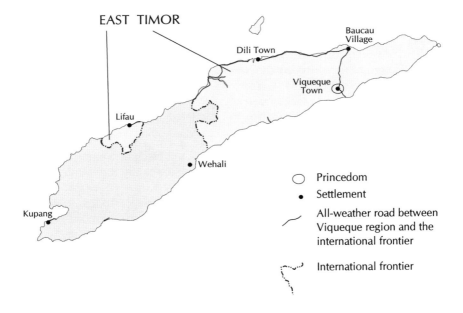

Figure 1.   East Timor

vessel approached, they saw in the ship a man garbed in a black cas-
sock, with a black beard, wearing a star on his forehead, and a golden
orb hanging down his chest. The queen ordered a councilor to ask the
stranger what he wanted. The stranger told his interpreter to inform
the population he had come to teach them the true words of God. The
queen and kings replied that the man's god was unknown to them and
that they wanted to have nothing to do with him. The stranger asked
permission for himself and his men to disembark, but the queen and
kings refused. The stranger then requested that they might at least be
permitted to collect water from a nearby spring. Permission was
granted. When the sailors jumped ashore they brought with them an
anchor that was attached by a chain to the ship, but the Timorese
failed to notice the attachment because they were preoccupied with
their great festival.

When the time came to depart, the signal was given to the crew, who
had by now returned to the ship. While the local people looked on,
the ship's captain knelt at the prow of the ship, put his hands together,
raised his eyes toward the sky, and at the proper moment, gave orders
for his people to set sail. The ship began to move away from the beach,
but then the ground beneath the Timorese also started to move. The
local populace was astonished as the ship moved into the waves, its
chain seeming as though it were taking the land with it! Every
Timorese ran toward the chain and did what he or she could to stem
the exodus of their land. Warriors slashed at it with their swords; others chewed betel to make a medicine that they might spit on the chain;
some begged the queen to help. But despite all these efforts the chain
did not part, and the ship seemed to continue pulling the land.

When the people had reached the pitch of trembling with terror their
leaders addressed the stranger, "Ah! Lord of the sea, lord of the deep
waters, lord of the beaches. Your Highness may go freely, but allow us
to remain, we and our land, in this place!" The stranger replied, "See-
ing that you do not wish to receive me and my people in your land
you could not possibly want to hear me speak of the World of God, so
now we wish to carry your land and you to our land." They replied,
"Your lordship can settle down on our land just so long as you don't
take us to your land."

The ship then stopped moving, ground to a stop, and with it the land.
The stranger disembarked, and the queen and the native priest moved
to greet him. The queen attempted to kiss his hand, but he abruptly
withdrew back his hand. "No! Do not come near me because I am a
sacred man!" Then they all exclaimed, "Great lord: you are a greater
sacred man than the greatest of our priests!" The kings gave the foreign
priest and his people a good reception. They even gave them a house in
which to live. The priest explained the doctrine of Lord God to the
queen of Lifau, and she and many of her subjects became Christians.

In 1556, on the neighboring island of Solor, the Portuguese established a Franciscan mission that incorporated a stone fort to protect recent converts made on Flores, an island just west of Solor, and as the years went by a population grew up around it. This population included the *mestiço* offspring of Portuguese soldiers, sailors, and traders from the Portuguese-controlled Malacca and Macau, who had married local women. In the years that followed, similar communities arose in eastern Flores and on Timor (Boxer 1960:350). These *mestiços* became known as the *topasses*.

Portuguese trading activities remained focused on Solor, and Portugal's presence on Timor remained superficial throughout the sixteenth and seventeenth centuries, the few Portuguese there being virtually all missionaries residing along the north coast. In 1568 their foothold became even more insecure. Dutch traders, also searching for sandalwood, landed at Kupang, the finest harbor in all of Timor and southwest of Lifau. The Dutch extended their influence over southwestern Timor with such rapidity that the Portuguese priests decided to strengthen their own presence.

Their counteroffensive involved a policy with a threefold purpose: (1) to keep Timor out of Dutch hands; (2) to bring the local kings under the Portuguese crown; and (3) to convert the Timorese to the Catholic faith. Their aim was clear enough, but its attainment was not unproblematic. From the beginning of the seventeenth century, the Dutch frustrated the Portuguese priests' proselytizing labors. Although ostensibly religious in nature, the missionaries were also the *de facto* representatives of the Portuguese government, and their failure to achieve their goals would have economic and political implications for the crown (Matos 1974:41, 47).

Missionary efforts made by the Dominican friars on Timor lagged a long way behind their successful efforts on Solor and in the easternmost part of Flores. It was not until the 1640s, when more chiefs had accepted Christianity and the overlordship of the Portuguese crown, that significant improvement was made on the earlier gains. The friars even moved into Kupang and started building a fort there. In 1653, before the friars could complete the fort, a Dutch force seized the settlement, expelled the friars, and from "Fort Concordia" (as Kupang was called) as their base, the Dutch embarked on a program to subdue the Atoni, the ethno-linguistic group dominant in western Timor, with the overall goal of monopolizing the sandalwood trade. In response, the friars summoned the *topasses* from Flores and Solor to help thwart Dutch efforts. The friars were successful to a certain degree, although Dutch traders visited villages along both the northern and southern coasts in search of sandalwood. The most popular port for Portuguese traders from Macau remained Lifau.

Even by 1661, when the Luso-Dutch treaty officially ended the fifty years of warfare between the Portuguese and the Dutch in the Eastern Archipelago, the Dominicans and *topasses* were the only Portuguese to

have permanent settlements on Timor (Boxer 1960:352). The Dominicans never had the resources to deploy more than five friars at any one
time, and in a country of rugged mountains and remote valleys, where
travel was arduous and slow—and was to remain so until well into the
twentieth century—these settlements advanced no further than the northern coastal plains (Matos 1974:19). The main center of missionary influence was in all likelihood restricted to the environs of Lifau. By the end of
the seventeenth century, while more Timorese had converted to Christianity, in most instances their conversions were more nominal than real,
and the indigenous people continued celebrating their traditional rituals.

The precolonial history of Timor is obscure. The "original" inhabitants of the island, one conjecture suggests, were the Atoni who may have
been displaced from their original territory in central Timor during the
fourteenth century by a later ethnic group coming from the west, the
Tetum-speaking peoples. These newcomers established themselves on the
fertile soils of the Benain Plain, in south central Timor, there to found a
kingdom known as Wehali kingdom (kingdom: *rai* [Tetum]; *reino* [Portu-
guese]).[2] Emigrants from Wehali then founded three new kingdoms in
central and eastern Timor, and the evidence tends to suggest they were
probably Liquiça, Suai, and Camenassa. Eventually many of the kingdoms assorted themselves among two great coalitions. One corresponded to what is now East Timor and was known variously as Liurai,
Belum, or Bellos, while the other coalition of kingdoms corresponded to
today's West Timor and was called Servião or Surviang. Its population
consisted almost entirely of Atoni-speaking people and its leader held the
title of Sonobai.

By the middle of the sixteenth century Timor is thought to have had
62 kingdoms, with 46 eastern kingdoms under the Belu and 16 western
kingdoms under the Servião. Each kingdom was headed by a chief
known as the *liurai*, whom the Portuguese referred to as the *régulo* or *rei*
(king). These kings, it seems, were more or less in a factitious state, fighting one another and forming and breaking military alliances as their
interests shifted. By the 1600s the reputation of Wehali as the most prestigious kingdom on the island was thoroughly established, but in 1642 a
Portuguese commander, Fernando Fernandes, defeated the Wehali army
and the psychological impact of this loss diminished the degree of defiant
confidence the kings had displayed toward the newcomers. Neither the
Portuguese nor the Dutch power however were strong enough to take
advantage of the weakened condition of the kingdoms that opposed them
and gain full control because they were handicapped by insufficient manpower and were, of course, fighting each other. Their mutual rivalry
obliged them to solicit support from the native rulers, a dependence that
was to keep the kings independent for upwards of another 250 years.

A succession of Portuguese viceroys, stationed in Goa, India, made half-hearted attempts to enforce the crown's jurisdiction over Timor during the second half of the seventeenth century, but as a practical matter the Dominicans were a sovereign body unto themselves. Backed by the *topasses*, they frustrated every effort made by the viceroy to impose regulations. The viceroy regularly griped about the friars' fierce determination to keep their independence, which brooked no opposition from the officials who held authority over them. The viceroy added immorality to his growing list of complaints against the friars and attempted to replace the Dominicans by Jesuits, a tactic the *topasses* countered by announcing they would permit only Dominican friars on Timor. "These are they who formerly taught our ancestors and forefathers and who at present teach us," they wrote to the viceroy in 1677, "We were brought up by them, and it is not right that we should abandon them and turn to others" (Boxer 1960:352). And that was that.

The impasse lasted until 1702 when, to gain a firmer grip, the viceroy appointed the first governor of the island who established a fort at Lifau. This proved to be the beginning of a national presence that endured (Boxer 1960:353) until 1975. The government was aided by the habitual incapacity, which continued during the eighteenth century, of the Timorese kings to present a common front to the foreigners. Indeed they expended most of their energy fighting one another. Even so, the Portuguese still could not extend their purchase on Timor much beyond Lifau because of the presence of the Dutch, who by now were irrevocably entrenched at Kupang. Added to this, the Servião kings persisted in launching sporadic attacks. Such was the low manpower of the Portuguese, never more than a hundred strong, that the kings almost succeeded in eradicating them. But the kings could never sustain their coalitions long enough to achieve their goal, and the governors at Lifau could always count on help from at least some of the Belu (Boxer 1960:353).

In 1719 a more dangerous chiefly federation began to challenge the Portuguese, an offensive that was to last, with intermissions, for more than fifty years. The catalyst was the onslaught by the Portuguese in November on the kings' mountain stronghold at Cailaco in the central region of the island and the bulk of the army consisted of 4,000 native militia. Although precipitous cliffs seemed to make the redoubt virtually impregnable, the Portuguese-backed forces succeeded in driving the rebels from one position to another, until it looked like the resistance of the indigenous population was about to be overcome. Just when the chiefs' army had been cornered on the summit, however, the wet season erupted in torrential downpours that made it impossible for the attackers to take the citadel.

Nor were the Dutch immune to attack, for in November 1749 the *topasses* attacked Kupang without warning, but in contrast to the Portuguese, the Dutch force succeeded in promptly slaughtering the attackers, thereby bringing most of western Timor under their jurisdiction (Boxer 1960:354). Success of this nature continued to elude the Portuguese, evidenced by the diluted character of the Portuguese presence on the island; by 1750, apart from several Dominican friars, the number of Portuguese had dipped to around seven, though it would increase somewhat over the course of the next few years. Added to the colony's woes were the viceroy's perennial complaints about the friars' sexual activities with the local women (Boxer 1960:354).

In 1768, with the backing of most of the kingdoms of Servião, the most prominent *topass* of the time, Francisco de Hornay, began a revolt against the Portuguese, and on 11 August 1769 the combined power of the rebels forced the evacuation from Lifau of 1,200 Portuguese and their supporters who sailed eastward until they found a suitable spot to reestablish themselves. On 10 October 1769, on a malaria-ridden harbor, they founded the settlement of Dili, which was to become the capital of Portuguese Timor (Felgas 1956:241). The Portuguese were no longer a presence in the west, where the Dutch were now firmly entrenched.

During the Napoleonic wars the English occupied Dutch Timor, as it was then known, though they were twice repelled at Kupang, one of the few Dutch forts to offer more than a token resistance (Boxer 1960:354–355). After the former Dutch possessions had been returned to the Netherlands in 1816, boundary disputes broke out between the Dutch and the Portuguese, and an attempt was made in 1850 to settle the squabbling. A former governor-general of Goa, Lopes de Lima, was appointed governor of Timor and plenipotentiary for the negotiations with the Dutch. In exchange for Maubara, an insignificant region just west of Dili, and an indemnity of 200,000 florins, he signed a convention ceding to the Dutch the important region of Larantuka on Flores and withdrew all Portuguese claims on Solor. The Dutch promptly took possession of Larantuka. Lisbon repudiated the agreement, and recalled Lopes de Lima in disgrace, but the damage had been done, for the Dutch retained Larantuka and Solor (Boxer 1960:355).

Boundary disputes in Timor soured the relations between the two European powers for the remainder of the nineteenth century until a series of meetings finally brought about a definitive settlement in the year 1913 (Boxer 1960:355), which divided Timor into the dual geopolitical units that persisted until the Republic of Indonesia invaded East Timor in 1975. Even under Indonesian rule, however, Timor remained for administrative purposes two separate units, and when East Timor became independent on May 20, 2002, the original duality was once more international.

The diplomatic accord reached in Europe and boldly inscribed in maps could not have been more at variance with the reality at grassroots level. Effective control by both colonial powers was restricted to a few localities dotted along the north coast, but elsewhere the kings continued to govern their small domains independent of any European meddling, their submission to the colonial governments marked only by having to pay a tribute to the two respective governors. In the case of the Portuguese it was this tribute that made it possible for them to maintain their presence on the island at all, since the Portuguese army was essentially comprised of the local militia of the kings, themselves commanded by a lieutenant-general chosen from among the lesser chiefs. This remained the only force the Portuguese administration had at its disposal in its campaigns against kings who might rebel (Thomaz 1977:21).

Governor António Francisco da Costa's attempt to impose tighter administrative supervision (involving a more effective method of collecting taxes) toward the end of the nineteenth century provoked a violent reaction from most of the kings who, in 1893 in Maubara, rebelled in what was to be only the first of a series of rebellions that proved a serious threat to Portugal and wrought destruction upon the rural areas (Dunn 1996:17). Timor was one of the last Portuguese colonies to be completely pacified, and the final pages were turned on kingly independence only with the appointment in 1894 of José Celestino da Silva who decided to subdue the kings once and for all. Although he would eventually prove to be the most effective of all the governors up to that time, his first two campaigns failed, and in reprisal Dom Boaventura, one of the rebel kings, whose base of operations was Manufahi (in the region of Same), ransacked Dili. Despite the massive manpower the governor was able to assemble—about 28 Europeans, some troops from Mozambique, and over 12,000 Timorese provided by kings loyal to the Portuguese—it took him until 1908 to achieve this goal. After it was achieved, though, the Portuguese could now consider the best way to administer their reluctant colony.

To make efficient civil administration possible, da Silva tightened his military organization by dividing Portuguese Timor into fifteen *commandos militares* or military commands, each administered from Dili (Felgas 1956:316), and implementing internal reforms complemented externally by a shift in the functioning governance. Instead of reporting to the Viceroy in Macau, as was previously done, the governor now reported directly to Lisbon. Even this strengthening of colonial power failed to intimidate the irrepressible Dom Boaventura, however, who in 1912 attempted yet another coup. It again failed, and its demise put to rest any plausible hope of independence the Timorese kings might entertain, because the attempted coup brought home to the administration just how dangerous a threat the kings still posed.

The Portuguese accordingly decided to undermine the kings' power base by abolishing their kingdoms and for good measure the office of king in virtually every part of Portuguese Timor. At the same time, they determined to establish a system of roads and bridges that would open up the regions of the interior, a venture that had actually begun under da Silva. The six years' administration of Filomeno da Camara, who became governor in 1911, established a network of roads and bridges that played a decisive part in the pacification of the country, for potentially troublesome regions such as Viqueque could now be more closely administered by the authorities. One result of the opening up of the interior was that it enabled Chinese merchants to expand from Dili into other parts of the colony where they established shops, an initiative that introduced the local Timorese populace to the idea of a market-oriented cash economy. However, as I saw for myself, even in 1967 this notion was still far from being put into practice, and Timor remained an overwhelmingly subsistence agricultural economy.

Beginning in January 1934 the military commands were gradually replaced by a system of civil units that the Portuguese called *circunscrições*, which formed the basis of the civil administration. Then, after two decades of tranquility, the history of Portuguese Timor was abruptly shattered when on 17 December 1941, and in defiance of the protests of Governor Ferreira de Carvalho, a force of 400 Dutch and Australian troops of the 2/2 Independent Company disembarked from the vessel "Soerabaja" and landed on a beach west of Dili in a pre-emptive action to thwart a presumed Japanese invasion. The Japanese government quickly responded by sending a thousand troops into Dili and 5,000 into Kupang, reinforcing them within a few days until the number of Japanese troops reached a total commitment of about 20,000 (Dunn 1996:19).

The Japanese unified Timor, even if only temporarily, as part of the Japanese "Greater Asia co-prosperity sphere." Some Australians remained fighting on the island and with the help of Timorese waged a guerilla war for many months. The devastation wrought on the local people, though, gave them a taste of what was to come later from the Indonesian occupation. Many hamlets were completely destroyed and thousands of people slaughtered before the Japanese succeeded in pushing the Australians off the island on 10 January 1943. Afterwards the Japanese mounted a massive retaliation into the hamlets and took even more Timorese lives.

As late as 1966 I discovered that anti-Japanese feelings still ran rife in Portuguese Timor, and André Pereira, a resident of Caraubalo, described with bitterness how the Japanese soldiers would simply chop down coconut trees when they wanted nuts and kill buffaloes and pigs without permission from their owners for meat. On other occasions, like the Portuguese and Dutch before them, the Japanese exploited the traditional rivalries between the various kingly families (Dunn 1996:22). Some families sided with the invaders and a few remained neutral, but the over-whelming majority opposed the Japanese.

The Japanese army surrendered at Kupang, which was the headquarters for the administration of the entire island, and the Japanese who were in Portuguese Timor were quickly moved across the former frontier into Dutch Timor. Unlike the people on Java and the other islands that were part of the Dutch empire, who had taken advantage of the occupation to proclaim independence, the Timorese showed no signs of wanting to take the opportunity to remove the Portuguese and appeared perfectly willing to return to their colonial condition. They freed not only their fellow Timorese who had been imprisoned by the Japanese but also the Portuguese prisoners from the concentration camps and quite spontaneously encouraged the reimposition of Portuguese administration. On 24 September 1945 on the waterfront of Dili the Japanese formally delivered the colony back to the Australians temporarily, and three days later a pair of Portuguese warships arrived on the shores of the capital. The final chapter of European rule was about to commence.

Portuguese Timor, therefore, remained in its colonial status, but as the result of concern about international image, the Portuguese government decided in the early 1950s to change the designation officially from "colony" to "overseas province," a legal fiction that continued until 1975.

In December 1975, after months of intrigue in the east, the Indonesian army crossed the frontier and invaded and subdued its minuscule neighbor, whose inhabitants thus found themselves under the control of yet another foreign power. The Indonesian occupation lasted until 1999 and effected many changes in the lives of the Timorese (chapter 7). However, the indigenous system of *sukus* (princedoms), *povoacões* (villages), and *knua* (hamlets) I observed in the 1960s was still functioning when I returned in 1999.

East Timor in 1966–1967

At the time of my fieldwork in 1966 and 1967 Portuguese Timor consisted of the whole eastern half of the island of Timor and a small enclave in the western half. The remainder of the western half was Indonesian territory. The number of major indigenous languages in Timor is at least 15, of which all but one—Atoni—are spoken in East Timor. Figure 2 shows the distribution of those having the most speakers. The Tetum-speaking people, who totaled about 150,000 in the late 1960s, may conveniently be classified into three subcategories: the Northern Tetum, the Southern Tetum, and the Eastern Tetum. The Northern and Southern groups are collectively known as the Western Tetum. Viqueque district falls within the Eastern Tetum

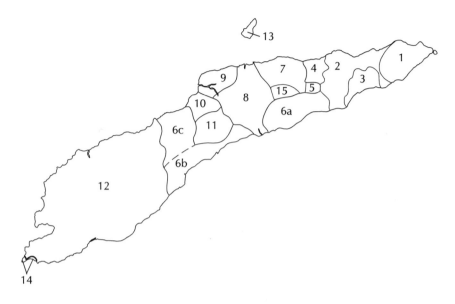

1	Fataluku	6	Tetum	6a	Eastern Tetum
				6b	Southern Tetum } Western Tetum
				6c	Northern Tetum
2	Makassai				
3	Nauhete	7	Galoli	10	Ema (Kemak)	13	Atauroan Languages
4	Uai Ma'a	8	Mambai	11	Buna'	14	Helong
5	Cairui	9	Tokodé	12	Mainly Atoni	15	Idaté

Figure 2.   Linguistic Regions of Timor

zone. The Tetum of this region refer to themselves as *ema fehan,* or the "people of the plain," and as such contrast themselves with the *ema foho,* or the "people of the mountains," preeminently the Makassai.

Administrative Structure

The Province of Timor is divided into ten *concelhos* or "districts," each of which is governed by an administrator who reports to the governor at Dili, the provincial capital.[3] These districts had replaced the former *circunscrições.* Each district consists of several *postos* or "subdistricts," each administered by a *chefe do posto* or subdistrict commissioner. One of these subdistricts (the *posto sede* or "subdistrict seat") serves as the seat of administration for the entire district, and this is where the administrator resides. Within it he also functions as subdistrict commissioner. Each subdistrict consists of a constellation of units called *sukus*, each administered by a *chefe de suku* or *liurai* who, as the chief of the *suku*, reports to the subdistrict commissioner. Each *suku* consists of a varying number of *povoacões* or villages (singular: *povoação*), each governed by a *chefe de povoação* or village headman. In the region where I carried out my fieldwork most villages consist of a varying number of dispersed settlements, consisting of anything up to a dozen or so houses *(uma)*, known as *knuas* (singular: *knua*) or hamlets, which are set apart from their neighbors by savanna and woodland. The *liurais,* and to a much lesser degree the headmen, represent the Portuguese administration to the local Timorese populace, and although the villagers elect them, their appointment must be ratified by the administration before they can assume office.

The term *suku* is a Malay word that is used throughout the archipelago, but with different, albeit overlapping, meanings depending upon locality. In Timor, as we have seen, it is a territorial unit within the Portuguese administrative system of governance, but the term also refers to a collection of clans that share the same traditions. The term is used throughout Timor, but in some regions the local population may employ alternative designations derived from their particular languages. In Caraubalo, one of the seven *sukus* making up the subdistrict seat of Viqueque district, this local alternative is *fukun*, a designation carrying the additional meaning of "node" or "point of articulation." There is no self-evident English translation of either *fukun* or *suku*, but in view of the fact that the indigenous unit denoted by these terms is a sub-unit of the traditional kingdom, the term "princedom" would seem as apt as any, and I shall adopt it here. It is at the level of the *suku* that European values interface most dynamically with indigenous ones.

With the dismantling of the kingdoms the *sukus* that composed them were left intact, and in many cases it was traditional *liurai* families who came to occupy the new office of *chefe de suku* that the administration created to run the *suku*. Today, the title *liurai* is used all over Portuguese Timor, but now it does not denote the head of a kingdom, that is, a confederation of *sukus*, but the more limited position occupied by the chief of a *suku*. Even so, the superior education of *liurai* families and the traditional prestige in which they are held typically means that a scion of *liurai* lineage usually occupies the influential position of *chefe de suku*, and while their influential range is limited to the *suku* rather than the kingdom *(rai)*, *liurais*—or rather, *liurai* families—continue to exercise political influence among the local population In Viqueque (figure 3), for example, all ten *chefes de suku* were of *liurai* stock, though some were more genealogically closer to the *liurai* family that had ruled the old Viqueque kingdom than others and therefore ranked higher in prestige. In Viqueque kingdom, before the office of *chefe de suku* had ever come into existence, Caraubalo *suku* was governed by a pair of indigenous figures known as the *makair fukun* (Mane Hat village) and the *dato ua'in* (Mamulak village). They were said to govern the *suku* jointly "as husband and wife govern the household, loving their dependents and respecting each other." Both were also headmen of their respective villages, and their offices have endured, with some erosion of their traditional authority, which has been arrogated to some degree by the Portuguese-backed office of *chefe de suku*.

The administrative center of Viqueque subdistrict is located in the town *(vila)* that bears the same name, Viqueque, the largest settlement in Viqueque district, and ranged around it are the ten *sukus* that comprise the subdistrict seat. One of these is the *suku* of Caraubalo, in which the town itself stands. Viqueque town is an undistinguished collection of buildings that include the administrator's house, the various offices of the administration, a school, an infirmary, and about half a dozen Chinese shops, as well as an assortment of other buildings that in different ways cater to the needs of the resident European and Chinese population. For the year or so that my wife and I lived in the area we resided in a former Chinese shop in Viqueque town, and from there visited the local hamlets each day.

Source: Junta de Investigações do Ultramar 1966

Figure 3.   The Region of Viqueque

First Days on the Island

Having now outlined the historical and ethnographic background to my fieldwork I want to say something about the circumstances of my research since these, of course, determined the kind of information I was able to obtain. To acquire a working knowledge of Portuguese and obtain official support for my visa applications my wife and I stayed in Lisbon from January to April of 1965 before returning to Britain to await our research visas, which were issued to us in December. We left London airport for Portuguese Timor on the afternoon of 2 February 1966.

We broke our journey with stops in India, Thailand, and Singapore, arriving at the Baucau airport on Wednesday, March 9, where we stayed at the inn in Baucau before traveling the 80 miles from Baucau to Dili by jeep and reporting our presence to the governor. Our trip, which we might have been able to undertake in five and one-half hours, was enlivened by two breakdowns, a flat tire, and an exacting fording of the River Manatuto on the north coast. Under the circumstances, the eight hours it took us to reach Dili at 5:30 P.M. were reasonable enough. During our visit to Dili we discovered that the only conceivable building available for our occupancy in Viqueque town was a rundown Chinese shop owned by a Dili-based trading company, and so we agreed to rent it. An architect, so we were promised, would visit Viqueque the following week to determine how much work would be necessary to make the building inhabitable. With this commitment we returned on March 30 to the inn in Baucau. On his way to Viqueque, the architect stopped at the Baucau inn on April 2, and invited us to travel with him next day to visit our future home, 42 miles and two hours away. When we arrived it was quite apparent that the building needed a great deal of refurbishing, and we returned to Baucau to wait for this to be done.

In Baucau I began ethnographic work among the local communities of Makassai-speaking people who resided in the region, and we spent a few days traveling around the far eastern part of the land thanks to a considerate Portuguese lieutenant who drove us there in his jeep. Our sojourn in Baucau gave us the opportunity to obtain medical supplies, baby food (our son was less than three months old), rolls of film, clothing, and other items unavailable in Viqueque. Since the inn was the destination for Australian tourists who came each Wednesday for a week's vacation, the friends we made there also sent us supplies from Australia after we became resident in Viqueque.

The work on our house dragged on for too long, so we decided to move into it regardless of its condition, and returned to Viqueque on June 2. Shortly after our arrival in the town the secretary to the administrator was kind enough to furnish me with a map of the home subdistrict and a list of its 52 villages (which were allocated among its ten *sukus*). *Liurai* Miguel da Costa Soares of Uma Ua'in Craik *suku*, the most respected of the ten *liurais* in the home subdistrict, supplemented what little information I had at the time by identifying the religious affiliation of each village. My intention was to work in a Tetum-speaking village that was predominately non-Christian, and his assessment was that only a few still remained—in the most distant Tetum *suku*, Bibileu. Eight hours' journey on horseback into hills that were also inhabited by the overwhelmingly non-Christian Makassai and Cairui-speakers, Bibileu certainly seemed isolated enough to fit my requirements.

Thus armed with this information, I made a request of the administrator, one of the most industrious in the colony, that he might arrange a house for me in Bibileu. On August 12 he was able to advise me I had one in a village called Hare Oan, and remarked that ten days later his administration would be carrying out its annual census of all ten *sukus* in the home subdistrict, and that its first destination would be Bibileu *suku*. I was welcome to accompany the four officials who would be making the trip on horseback up into the *suku*.

A census team spends as much time in each of the ten *sukus* as is necessary to complete its survey, which involves the inspectors collecting information about his wealth from each male adult and, if he is married, about his dependents. They carry out their survey in the hamlet of the *suku* where its *liurai* resides. Depending on the size of the population, the data collection may take as few as three hours or as many as fifteen. A *suku* with a large population may keep a team busy at the *liurai*'s residence for the better part of two days. Bibileu is the home subdistrict's fourth largest *suku*, which meant that my team spent a night—August 22—there, with me helping in their secretarial work but also adding my own queries as each Timorese man walked up to our table: "What is your religion? What language do you speak?"

Religion was my criterion of acculturation, and by the time the horses were mounted to take the team to the next *suku*, that of Uai Mori, my personal survey had already established that the Tetum-speaking population of Bibileu *suku* was far more Christianized than I had been given to understand. So I decided to find out for myself just what the relationship between religion and language in the whole of the home subdistrict really was. I asked the secretary if I might accompany the team to Uai Mori, and he gave his consent with the result that I was fortunate enough to have the experience of traveling all over the entire subdistrict in the following couple of weeks and make a comparative evaluation of religion and language in all its *sukus*. When I returned home after the final excursion, I decided that before going to Hare Oan I would spend a couple of days sifting through my data to assure myself that this far-off village really suited my needs best.

The analysis showed that the information I had been given in Viqueque town before my excursions had not been entirely accurate. It seemed that of the five predominately Tetum-speaking *suku*s in the home subdistrict, that is, Caraubalo *suku*, Uma Ua'in Craik *suku*, Balarauain *suku*, Uma Kik *suku*, and Bibileu *suku*, it was not Bibileu that was the least Christianized, but Caraubalo itself. And among its six Tetum-speaking villages, those of Mamulak and Mane Hat actually had fewer Christians than non-Christians. The administrator consented to help me get a house in one of these two villages, and so for a few weeks I looked on my daily expeditions into the Caraubalo hamlets abutting Viqueque town as an interim period while my second request was being processed. But as it happened, all my fieldwork was to be conducted from our Viqueque town house since, for whatever reason, a residence in Mane Hat or Mamulak never came about, perhaps because communications between the Caraubalo *liurai* and the administrator broke down somewhere, or perhaps the administrator thought I might change my mind again. During the time I was carrying out my fieldwork, therefore, I used to walk, usually with my wife, each day from our house to the hamlets, to spend a morning or afternoon, and sometimes the evening, talking with the people there.

Living inside a village would certainly have helped us acquire a knowledge of the Tetum language more speedily, and in a community in which some members proved to be suspicious about our intentions, we would in all likelihood have been more rapidly and thoroughly accepted as participants in village life. Yet perhaps things turned out for the best. There were advantages to living outside the community. First, we were better able to safeguard our health and that of our son since I suspect the daily regime of hygiene we imposed on our servant and maid in Viqueque would not have been as feasible in a hamlet. Secondly, virtually everyone—at least at the beginning of our fieldwork (my wife helped me with much of my data collecting among the Timorese women)—was reticent when faced with our ethnographer's notebook, and in the privacy of our own house, I could write up my notes undisturbed at the end of each day.

Field Research

Our pattern of research developed a life of its own. In September and October my wife (when she was not preoccupied with our son) and I would leave the house and tramp along the paths linking the hamlets, hoping to find a person willing to converse with a stranger whose command of Tetum was barely even elementary. At that time of year men were burning off the debris that had accumulated in their gardens over the previous year and mending fences, but since few people understandably had the patience to talk to me, I spent hours wandering alone, a period during which I was at least able to construct maps of the area. My strategy was to ask anyone who was willing to talk to me his or her name and village and the names of any prominent topographic features, but no sustained contact was forthcoming until one afternoon.

I was strolling through a hamlet I later found out was called Cailulik with a Timorese soldier stationed in Viqueque town when I happened on some people eating a meal in an open-sided, makeshift hut. My companion inquired in Tetum what was going on. A fourteen-year-old boy sitting nearby jumped to his feet and told him the meal celebrated the final stage in the rites of death for a resident of the hamlet who had been buried twelve months earlier. Issuing us an invitation to eat with the company, he identified himself as José Pereira and told my friend he lived in the nearby hamlet of Baria Laran. During the meal that followed he brought me into the picture by asking my companion who I was and what was the nature of my business in Caraubalo. The question was phrased in Tetum, but I was able to understand what he said, so I replied in Portuguese on the assumption that he had had some schooling (unlike most Timorese), and learned some Portuguese, explaining my reasons for coming to Timor. José, I thought at the time, found it difficult to take my reply seriously, and many weeks later he asked me why a foreigner would interest himself in studying an obscure language and the customs of its speakers? I later learned that he had been educated by Christian missionaries in a high school in Dili and had assimilated certain of the missionaries' attitudes, as had many of the other educated younger people I later talked to in Viqueque.

As the weeks passed, José and I became constant companions, and I believe his interest in my research caused him to avoid school more than he might otherwise have been tempted to do. I think José may have come to regard the work I was trying to do as having some value. That first afternoon he had told me his father, André Pereira, whose Timorese name was Naha Funok, would welcome us in his house in the nearby hamlet of Baria Laran. Could we go there tomorrow? He would be happy to call at our house and show my wife and me the way. "And don't forget your camera!" he was quick to add.

As we were to learn the next day, the forty-two-year-old André had received some European education before its course was disrupted by the Japanese invasion of 1942; he had, as I recounted earlier, unhappy memories of events during the war years, which he believed prevented him from making a place for himself in the world beyond his village. Still, his few years at school had equipped him to converse confidently with members of the administration, and over the years officials had become accustomed to use André rather than the official headman when they wanted to communicate their policies to the Mamulak residents. Thus André's political influence was increased and his social prestige enhanced. His respect was generally high among other villagers, too, and he generously gave his time and presents liberally to other villagers.

The next day José led us to his father's house, where André, his wife Hílda, and the rest of his household had gathered to greet us. We talked, ate pork and green vegetables, and drank wine. Because my command of the Tetum language was still rudimentary we talked in Portuguese—the last time I used that language with a villager; from that day on all my conversations, even with André, were held in Tetum. As the afternoon lengthened into evening, we took our leave. In our house that night I wrote down what my wife and I could recall of André's talk on life in Mamulak village. It covered six and a half pages in my notebook.

We later discovered that André had increased his social standing as a result of our visit, so I was able to consider our talk a fair exchange of benefits. Luckily for my research, André had plenty of social rivals who did not want to be outshone, so now that André had broken the ice, invitations began to come in. Our visits to the hamlets multiplied so encouragingly I quickly filled a notebook. Later I switched to my typewriter.

One individual who was always a ready provider of information was thirty-five-year-old Agostinha Soares of Mane Hat village. In contrast to most women of her age Agostinha had remained single. She had a sociable personality and was forever active in communal life. Of all the villagers she was the least concerned by our first excursions to village homes, and we were fortunate to become firm friends with her. Agostinha's popularity drew us into an ever-expanding network of people, and before long we were part of the local scene. Agostinha loved introducing us to different features of village life and loved the limelight. My wife and I were surprised after we had left Timor and examined the portfolio of photographs we had taken to find her face cropping up so many times—an indication of the interest our presence had for her.

Although I discovered some Tetum individuals who appeared more interested in discussing their ritual lives than did their colleagues, and I talked with some who professed to more knowledge than most villagers, in the majority of cases I discovered that when they provided me with information, they would appeal to the jurisdiction of narrative. Tetum oral tradition was a major way by which knowledge of ritual and spiritual matters were transmitted from generation to generation. Myths were usually the literary agencies here, and anecdotal incidents of a much more personal character were also commonly brought forth as authoritative sources of information; legends and folktales were used less for this purpose.

Ideas concerning immortality, souls, spirits, the destination of the soul of the deceased, and the origins of humanity were not constituents of anything resembling a systematic set of cosmological notions. Instead, their contexts were invariably literary, and in describing them or using them to provide an explanation for some aspect of ritual behavior people would resort to reciting the appropriate literary texts in which these ideas were contained. There was not, to put the matter another way, anything resembling an indigenous theology. Instead of a grand cosmological schema gradually being revealed to me as I accumulated answers to my questions, what I in fact acquired was an assortment of fractured and often uncoordinated items of information, most having their origins in narratives. Although Émile Durkheim's definition of religion has much relevance for the Caraubalo Tetum (cf. chapter 2), his insistence on the attribution "unified system of beliefs and practices" might be considered too stringent a criterion for the beliefs and practices I describe in this book.

The absence of a systematic set of cosmological notions was matched by an absence of ritual exegesis. People enacted ritual rather than explaining it. Inconsistencies in the manner in which the same ritual would be carried out were common, especially in the death ritual, which was the most frequently performed public ritual. No one apparently could account for these inconsistencies any more than they claimed that any norms were being violated by them.

Even individuals who played leading roles in ritual offered little more exegetical insight than those less interested, but such interpretations, as they were, constituted little more than verbal descriptions of the actions. Nor did I learn of persons so adept in arcane matters that they could be properly described as theological specialists. Such persons, I should add, may have been present in Viqueque, but if they existed they most definitely escaped my acquaintance. The local populace's disinterest in explaining their ritual lives means that the portrait I paint in these pages is a composite fashioned from fragments of indigenous thoughts conveyed in response to my questioning numerous individuals.

Persons who provided me with information often contradicted not only others, but also, on occasions, even themselves. Apparently contradictions abounded in the oral texts themselves as well as between the texts and statements I received. For example, in certain narratives the names "Rubi Rika and Lera Tiluk" appear as those of two different persons, whereas in at least one other narrative they are apparently assimilated into a single personage. In much the same fashion, the succession followed by incumbents in the political office of *makair fukun* is given differently in narrative from listings given to me by persons in Caraubalo. The absence of a ready-made indigenous catechism forced me into what I consider to be a typical—though perhaps not readily acknowledged—role of the ethnographer, that of ethnographic theologian. It should be clear from this characterization that the following representation of "Tetum religion," although it might meet Durkheim's stipulation, is a much more systematic formulation than any Caraubalo villager would make. As in many other ethnographer's accounts my representation draws very much on my own interpretation of how its practitioners organized their experience of life and what value they ascribed to their actions.

I would suggest, therefore, that for the participants the main point to the rituals carried out in Caraubalo lies in the realm of performance rather than in that of hermeneutics, what Edward Muir (1997:168) defines as "the process of discerning meaning." Now that we have touched on some of the various forms the ritualization of reproduction takes in Tetum society, one question that might reasonably be asked is whether the behavior conventional at rites of passage, and on other occasions when spirits are evoked, is in fact little more than mere performance devoid of meaning. In describing the development of Christianity in Europe Muir (1997:7–8) called attention to what he identified as a change in attitude that revolutionized the way people came to think about the nature of ritual. He argues that prior to the advent of Protestantism, ritual was credited with the capability of literally consummating physical transformations: in the Catholic Mass, for example, the bread was thought to be substantially transformed into Christ's body. The Protestant revolution interpreted this "transformation" as symbolic. It served only to remind congregation members of Christ's sacrifice on the Cross

In the matter of the Tetum interpretation of ritual efficacy we need first to contrast the perspective of the social anthropologist and that of the historian. The latter can glean some insight into how religious thinkers regard the nature of their religion by studying their written words, whereas societies lacking such specialists as well as a literary tradition cannot offer this help to the ethnographer. At the same time, ethnographic fieldwork affords the ethnographer the opportunity denied the historian. He or she witnesses at firsthand ritual behavior and has the opportunity to assess its meaning by inquiring among the participants what it is they think they are doing and how they feel about it. In Caraubalo, however, the ambiguity and contradictions of participants' responses were not as helpful as I had anticipated, with the result that it is not possible for me to affirm that the participants in the rituals thought their actions were in some ways bringing about changes in the world of experience or whether, instead, they regarded them as symbolic statements about that world. The impression I received from questioning participants and observing what they did was that some individuals seemed quite convinced about the reality of the world beyond the senses whereas others were almost agnostic, seeming to engage in ritual because that was the socially accepted—and expected—way to behave.

Nevertheless, whatever degree of credulity or indifference each person might bring to his or her participation in the ritual life, the fact is that collective rituals among the Tetum are performed as though the community has a purpose in performing them that is more than simply expression; the recurring purpose is to bring life to the community. Hocart (1970:33 [1936]) phrased this idea in the following way: "We can only note that, like the concept of life, the technique of life-giving exists all the world over. Everywhere man goes through prescribed forms of words and actions in the persuasion that he can thereby transfer life from one thing to another." No matter how participants construe their actions, as we shall see, it is Tetum ritual that transfers life from ghosts to kin and in so doing confers life on the ghosts themselves.

Endnotes

[1] An excellent analysis of the notions of spirit and matter in another ethnic group in the East Indies can be found in R. H. Barnes' (1974) study of the Kédang, who live on the neighboring island of Lembata.

[2] For ethnographic studies of Wehali see Francillon 1967 and Therik 1995.

[3] I am employing the "ethnographic present" to describe the administrative system of Portuguese Timor as it was during my period in the field, and for the remainder of this account of Tetum life in 1966–1967 will continue to do so, i.e., until the final chapter.

Chapter 2

The World of Spirits

Émile Durkheim, it will be recalled, defined religion as "a unified system of beliefs and practices relative to sacred *[sacré]* things—that is to say things separated and forbidden—beliefs and practices that unite into a single moral community, called a church, all those who adhere to them" (Durkheim 1960:65; my translation). "Sacred things," in Durkheim's view, were things fundamentally separate from things (including persons) that were in the opposite, yet complementary, category of "profane," or what I would also refer to as "secular," a distinction he took to be absolute, allowing no gradations. For Durkheim human thought conceptualized no pair of categories as profoundly differentiated or so radically opposed. This absolute quality that he attributed to the distinction between sacred and profane has been discredited (cf. Lukes 1985, *passim*), but less extremely regarded, this contrast gives us insight into Tetum collective ideas, for it is this distinction that is fundamental to their way of classifying experience. Indeed, the contrast the Tetum make between two of their most symbolically charged terms, *lulik* and *sau* (the verbal form) or *saun* (the adjectival), matches fairly closely Durkheim's proposition.[1]

Edward E. Evans-Pritchard (1951:80) has written that "the most difficult task in anthropological fieldwork is to determine the meanings of a few key words, on an understanding of which the success of the whole investigation depends. . . ." The categories *sau* and *lulik* are just such "key words" in the Tetum language. *Lulik* can be translated as "to prohibit," "to be prohibited," "to be impeded (by rites or laws)," "ceremony," "animistic rite," "that which is sacred, venerated, untouchable," "prohibited," "impeded," and "holy" and is used in innumerable verbal constructs such

25

as *buat lulik*, "sacred thing." Some dictionaries even translate the term as "witchcraft," "magic power," "enchantment," and "pagan idol," although these are misleading referents.[2] The Tetum language has various ways for suggesting the notion of prohibition, such as *hakahik* or *bandu*, but these tend to be applied in what might be called secular or profane contexts rather than where the sense of the spiritual or supernatural is being evoked. For this reason some writers have characterized *lulik* as the religion of the Timorese, or else, more restrictedly perhaps, as a "cult" (Pascoal 1949:12–15). Educated Catholic Timorese sometimes refer pejoratively to the indigenous religion as the religion of *lulik*, and insist that the *"luliks"* are the objects of prayer, though this is not the case.

Connotations of *lulik* would appear to correspond quite well with Durkheim's *sacré*, as standing for something "set apart" or "forbidden," and I found that the term *lulik* was invariably used with a connotation that implied that the speaker was making some reference to something that was quite alien to everyday reality. In virtually all contexts it implied a spiritual component or a component that could be described as extraordinary. *Lulik*, to put it another way, is used in situations where something bordering or beyond the reach of empirical reality is under consideration. Thus a person who carries out rituals on behalf of his or her community may be referred to as a *dato lulik* or *na'in lulik*, the adjective *lulik* here being added to the terms for aristocrat and lord respectively, that is, designations that by themselves carry no implications of the extraordinary. As another example, whereas the term *uma* is the generic term for building, modified by the term *lulik*, as in *uma lulik*, it denotes the ritual house of a descent group, a repository for the group's sacred emblems.

At the same time, it would be going all together too far to translate the term *lulik* as broadly as "religion" or "cult," as such an authority on Timorese culture as Pascoal has done, even though to my knowledge these English language terms have no correspondences in Tetum. However, there is nothing the least surprising about this since, as I pointed out previously, what one might characterize as Tetum "religion" is really an amalgam of fragmented notions, many of which neither cohere with one another nor have much direct bearing on ritual life. Nevertheless, certain connections between ritual and idea are made where they can be identified by the analyst and these links do make it possible to represent Tetum ideas and practices as something more than simply an uncoordinated collection of ethnographic items. One way a semblance of coherence can be made discernible is by taking advantage of three processes by which Tetum collective thought organizes categories: disjunction, conjunction, and analogy.

Lulik's counterpart, *sau*, can be translated as "to lift a prohibition," "to dispense from an obligation," "to exempt," "free (of an obligation)," "permitted," "not prohibited." The term *sau* is used with other terms to qualify them in the way *lulik* is used, as in *sau batar,* which denotes the ritual performed before the corn *(batar)* is harvested, and which makes the corn available for profane or secular use.

The profane or secular world *(rai)* is the habitat of human beings, and it rests atop the sacred underworld. Visible and tangible, the secular world is ordered by traditional conventions that are transmitted from one generation to another through the agency of men. Women, of course, play a major part in life's transactions, but their authority is linked with reproductive forces of this underworld, which is the domain of the sacred. As in the domain of the profane, the sacred world contains (ghostly) kin of both sexes, but to the extent that the villagers conceptualize it, this world is more closely associated with women than men. The Tetum name for this world is *rai laran* or "inside world," which is identified as a female god, called *rai inan*, literally, "mother earth," a nurturing, caring, deity.

When asked to clarify some obscure point of information about this feminine subterranean world, individuals to whom I spoke relied on the authority of spoken tradition, which itself is derived from their oral literary traditions, for their information. Therefore, before I describe the nature of the unseen world as people in Caraubalo represented it to me, I present a brief account of this aspect of Tetum culture to help us understand more thoroughly how deeply "Tetum religion" depends for its integrity on their literary art forms.

The Power of Words

Tetum oral literature provides the culture with its most imaginative outlet, and although its narratives, poetry, and ritual language cannot be regarded as constituting a liturgical body of texts that could be described as a sacred canon, these literary creations, as I indicated earlier, form a prime repository of ideas regarding the sacred realm and ritual.

The Tetum language contains a number of literary categories, some of which correspond to those used in English. The term *lia tuan*, for example, can be glossed as "legend." As in the English language, its usage refers to events in the far-distant past that while often portrayed in extraordinary terms nonetheless suggest some underlying historical plausibility. Tales describing the peopling of Timor by seafarers arriving from the western islands (see below) would be classed as *lia tuan*; whereas, in contrast, another category of narrative called *aiknananoiks* corresponds more to what we would characterize as "myths," "folktales," "fables," "morality tales," or "just-so stories." Accounts of how the first inhabitants ascended out of holes in the ground, for instance, or the entertaining adventures of Monkey and Crocodile, and the fabulous interactions between people and apparitions from the sacred world would be assigned to this indigenous category. Although these stories are not classed as male property or a secret masculine verbal resource closed to the scrutiny of women, only men tell them in public.

Narrators who command an unusually rich repertoire of tales may earn the prestigious title of "lord of the word," and on public occasions such as marriages they may be called on to demonstrate their skill. Those *aiknananoiks* that impart a mythological slant to the past are thought to have come down the generations essentially unchanged and cannot, as José Pereira informed me one day, be "made up." The same is true of *lia tuan*, but myths are invested with a proprietary quality the former lack. Whereas *lia tuan* may be held as part of a common tradition by several communities, myths tend to be more exclusive to descent groups and other self-contained social collectivities since they typically provide literary justification for certain jural or ritual rights to which they lay claim. It should go without saying therefore that invention is not a quality the Tetum associate with myths. Nor, for that matter, does creativity enjoy much appreciation in stories of any kind. Certainly, there are plot and character variations in the nonmythic *aiknananoiks*, and I collected numerous variants of the same plot, but even so individuals reciting these stories generally prefer to stick closely to conventional renderings.

Whereas *aiknananoiks* of a mythological cast are a nocturnal variety of verbal art—reciting them in daylight is *lulik*—a second category of literature known as *aiknananuks* may be voiced during the day or night. This category of literature consists of poems and songs that unlike myths can be invented for immediate circulation. *Baba fuan* or "fruit of the drum" is a subcategory of this genre and it consists of verses usually recited by women to the accompaniment of drums in dances. Tetum-speakers have an extensive number of these *baba fuan* and they like to contrast their prolific repertoire with the paucity of the Makassai repertoire, which they claim have only four or five *baba fuan*. They give as their reason the fact that the rhythm of the words eludes the unsubtle notes of the large drums and gongs played by the Makassai. Some *baba fuan* have special purposes. For example, women direct *moru ema* or "songs of poison" as barbs at adulteresses as a form of public insult, and you hear them when women and men are performing the *lisu*, which is a circular dance common all over East Timor. *Baba fuan* are described as *aiknananuk moris* (*moris* = alive), which Agostinha Soares characterized as "happy" songs women could sing on any occasion.

Other songs, which she identified as "unhappy" since they are sung only during a death ritual, are also of considerably more ritual significance. The term for them is *mate lia* (the words of death that are uttered only on the occasion of the death ritual) or, more formally, *metan do don* (*metan* = dark, black; *don* = to keen as you reflect on the deceased). Because of their sacred connotations, death words resemble some *aiknana-noiks* in that their utterance is invested with power, and reciting them outside this ritual is *lulik*. The two taboos differ in their respective natures, however, because the sanction against reciting a story during daylight is a vaguely defined notion of bad luck, whereas reciting the words of death carries the sanction of death. It is hardly any wonder then that women were rather reluctant to recite for our benefit the words of these *mate lia* or even to play the drumbeats that accompany them. Agostinha Soares, fortunately for my ethnography, seemed not in the least inhibited. "I'm not afraid of the songs," she once remarked—however, even she avoided reciting them within the hearing distance of her friends and neighbors.

During the funeral, as I describe in detail in chapter 6, the *mate lia* are sung on various occasions, such as when the mourners are removing the corpse from the hamlet to the cemetery and outside the house of a person who has just died. In the latter context, men join women so that both sexes are united in the face of death. The women, however, lead the performance, in a style of singing called *simu* (to give; to receive) in which they sing one line of the *mate lia*, and their male partners respond with their own line. This form of parallel ritual speech is widespread over the archipelago, and in Tetum occurs in all public and many private rituals. Among the public rituals in which they play an important part is marriage, where they are known as *lia moris* or "words of life." They, too, bear a more formal designation, *nassak ho solo* or "to be happy."

Myths of Origin

Although the residents of Caraubalo have several different narratives from which to select when they account for their presence in the region, the history of the Tetum-speaking peoples of Viqueque remains indistinct, and we have no way of knowing how their rituals and beliefs originated. The majority of Tetum-speaking peoples reside in central Timor, and their oral traditions, as I noted earlier, describe them as having come from the west by boat, settling in Wehali, and displacing an earlier population of non-Austronesian people who are thought to have occupied the entire island at that time. Assuming there is some historical validity to these accounts, since they then spread eastward into what was to become Portuguese Timor, one might reasonably suppose the present Tetum of Viqueque are the descendants of an immigrant population that also displaced the (non-Austronesian) Makassai, who reside adjacent to the eastern Tetum along the southern plain and northwards in the mountains.

Rather more imaginative myths in Caraubalo include a story that tells how Timor came into existence.

> The narrative describes how a sacred queen *(liurai feto lulik)*, who had two children, Oha Taluk and Bui Taluk, was one day weaving the sea as an ordinary woman might weave a piece of cloth, except that in her case the thread was made up of clouds that dangled down from the sky. This sea-cloth became very long and the queen became increasingly vexed by one of her brood who kept playing around her and distracting the queen from her work. Several times she told the child to stop its antics, but the child continued playing. Eventually the mother was so exasperated she struck out at the child with her shuttle, missed, and inadvertently cut the cloth into two parts, which is how the single sea became divided into two, the female sea to the north and the male sea to the south, with the island of Timor in between.

Several other myths told in Viqueque recount what is supposed to have happened in those primeval times when the order that now governs society and the supernatural world was created. The myths identify various alternative locations as the origins of humanity—a pregnant stone, the rear room of the house, the womb of a buffalo cow, and the underworld—but their invariable element is the emergence of human beings in mythic times from some womb-like receptacle. The version people seem to tell the most identifies the origin of the earliest population *(rai na'in* or landlords) of Caraubalo with the earth itself. The following is a summary of the myth.[3]

> Sometime after the island of Timor came into being a vent called Mahuma appeared on the surface of the land and from it climbed a pair of brothers, Rubi Rika and Lera Tiluk, and their sister, Cassa Sonek, who as first comers claimed the land that is now Caraubalo. Their descendants, who now reside in Mane Hat and Mamulak villages, became in the course of time the aristocrats *(datos)* and landowners *(rai na'in)* of Caraubalo *suku*. Rubi Rika, Lera Tiluk, and Cassa Sonek were followed out of the vent by other people. The descendants of these people became commoners and tenants of the three siblings, and they founded descent groups that today inhabit the four other Tetum-speaking hamlets of Caraubalo.

In the figurative language used in ritual speech the commoners are referred to as the *mahan no leu* or "people who sit in the shade." This is a metaphorical expression related to the fact that at council meetings and other meetings at which representatives of all the Caraubalo villages gather, the commoners sit outside the main part of the council building in the shade of the overhanging roof sheltered from the sun. The aristocrats of Mamulak and Mane Hat *(datos* who are figuratively known as the *batar no katin)* remain inside the building, and like the building are said to shade the *mahan no leu* from the sun. In this context it might be worth noting that the seventh village in Caraubalo, Sira Lari, the Makassai-speaking community, is figuratively entitled the *taka tan tabir*, which is a ritual term used to denote an orphan, because its members came from outside Caraubalo *suku*—from a location called Balakik—and, like a stranger being "accepted and brought up by a family," they were given a home by the Tetum population of the *suku*.

The myth therefore serves to justify the social prerogatives of contemporary social groups, including a status hierarchy in which aristocrats *(datos)* are superior to the commoners *(ema rai)*, or, put in an alternative idiom, the *batar no katin* are superior to the *mahan no leu* and the *taka tan tabir*. Indeed, some indication of the importance of the *batar no katin* in the *suku* of Caraubalo may be gauged from the fact that this expression is an alternative to another figure of speech by which the population of Mane Hat and Mamulak is known, namely, *inan no aman* or "mother and father" of the *liurai* himself. The narrative also establishes the idea that the founders of Caraubalo originally emerged from out of the ground, a primeval exit denoted by the term *sai rai* or "to leave the earth," which is used for the birth ritual. The Mahuma vent is also called *fona*, some of whose referents include "hole" or "vagina," and is a pathway into the body of the earth goddess that connects the sacred world with the secular world.

The semantic associations of the mother goddess are elaborate. In the Tetum language the term *lolon* refers to various kinds of cavities, including the womb and the interior space of a room, associations that converge in the aforementioned notion of *rai laran* or "interior of the earth," which is not only the place of origin of the autochthonous population of Caraubalo but is of course also the domicile of the spirits. Another designation for mother earth is *rai lulik* or "sacred world," though the term is also used for more restricted locales, such as a plot of land that is regarded as *lulik* because it is the property of a nature spirit (see below). The wombs of women and buffaloes, the rear compartment of the family house, and certain stones (called "pregnant stones") are used in different ritual contexts to symbolize the *rai lulik*, usages that suggest that childbirth, the birth of buffalo calves, and the birth of "baby stones" from the "mother stone" correspond in a symbolic sense to the primeval emergence of the three founding ancestors, Rubi Rika, Lera Tiluk, and Cassa Sonek, from the great vent, Mahuma.

The Sacred World

The body of *rai inan* is home to several different agencies of a spiritual nature, each of which is regarded as possessing *lulik* qualities and the authority to be either a help (if suitably approached) or a hindrance to human beings. Especially important to humanity is their power over human procreation since the fertility of the two sexes is thought to originate in the world of *lulik*, and the influence they bring to bear over harvests and the procreation of animals. It may be that these elementals derive their powers from the nurturing authority of the earth mother rather than being themselves authors of it, but whatever the ultimate source, they have considerably more immediate involvement with human beings than does the earth deity herself. By using rituals as a means of tapping the generative powers of each spiritual agency, human beings empower themselves into bringing not only new life but also abundance in many forms into their world.

Although the contrast between the spirit world and the human world is most typically conceptualized by the Tetum-speakers as one between an underworld and an upperworld, that is, in a vertical dimension, it may at times also be thought of as a horizontal axis, for things that are *lulik* have the capacity to intrude into human space. Animals, trees, rock formations, streams, waterfalls, and such natural objects that pertain to the world outside the hamlet can each possess the quality of *lulik*, which is typically attributed to unusual events described in local myths or legends, or to the objects' unusual appearance.

The contrast between the world of *sau* and the world of *lulik*, therefore, finds expression in Tetum imagination as one between the hamlet and the wilderness. This contrast is represented in oral narratives as one between the land of Timor itself and some alien land located on the other side of the sea, and a common plot found in these narratives describes a man leaving his homeland to travel across the sea, performing heroic feats, and returning transfigured in some miraculous way. Status transformation also occurs in stories featuring a hero who descends to the bottom of a river, lake, or the sea, and eventually returns endowed with an entirely different persona. Because the uncultivated wilderness that surrounds the cultivated landscape of gardens is imaginatively linked with the sacred world, travelers through it usually walk guardedly lest they encounter manifestations from the *rai lulik*, entanglements that provide *aiknananoiks* with one of their most popular themes. They also furnished informants with responses to my questions about the spirit world and its denizens.

Conceptions of Divinity

As we have seen, the earth is literally spoken of as "mother earth" or *rai inan*, but people are unclear about whether the goddess is a spiritual entity who has established her residence below the surface of the land or whether she is the earth itself, as the Tetum male deity may be identified with the sun. Because her name "mother earth" implies as much, I think she is probably thought of in this way, a possibility rendered all the more likely because of the "vagina" attributed to the earth. If this is the case, then she would also identify with the *rai lulik* and be the ultimate source of fertility and of life, an identification that accords well with the implication that the earth goddess nurtures human beings and satisfies their needs through the agency of the other spirits, for she does not do so directly herself. Although some of these spirits share certain qualities (e.g., all have powers human beings lack), we may thus conceive of them as being distinctive aspects of this female deity herself rather than independent entities existing in their own right. Ritual behavior involving them, then, may be seen as an indirect attempt to evoke specific attributes of the goddess. These spirit refractions of the earth goddess are the nature spirits of the land *(rai na'in)* or "lords of the land"; the nature spirits of water *(u'e na'in)* or "lords of the water"; and various spiritual entitles *(klamar)* that nurture buffaloes, corn, and rice. Also residing below the surface of the land are two other spiritual entities, the ghosts of the ancestors *(mate bein)* and the souls of individuals recently deceased *(klamar mate)*. These are not regarded as aspects of *rai inan*, and they exist in their own right.

Maromak

A passive, masculine divinity that dwells in the sky and among the clouds, *nai maromak*, or more simply, *maromak*, is said by villagers of Caraubalo to have intervened in human affairs on one occasion only. This was when he impregnated the earth mother and thereby brought the first people, namely, those who emerged from the ground, into existence. Since that primeval moment, the male deity has shown scant concern for his human progeny, and they reciprocate with disinterest. *Maromak* may well be embodied in the sun, which is said to have been in mythological times inclined at a lower angle in the sky than it is today until an elder lifted it up into its present position.

Tetum-speaking populations in other regions of Timor are described by ethnographers as displaying more involvement with *maromak*. Vroklage (1952:11) reports that the Northern Tetum pray to *maromak*, and while remarking that *maromak* is too remote for people to turn to frequently, another ethnographer states that in the past before going to war men used to bathe themselves in his honor and when uttering ritual oaths would evoke his name (Wortelboer 1955:290). Tom Therik (1995:234) reports that in Wehali "the Tetum do not differentiate Maromak from ancestors. For them, their ancestors are the Maromak." I did not find this to be the case at all in Caraubalo, where *maromak* and the ancestors or ghosts *(mate bein)* are quite distinct concepts that allow no merging.

Other Spiritual Agencies

The land, which as we have seen is closely identified with the mother goddess, is also an integral element of the Timorese own self-identity. As I pointed out earlier, the residents of Caraubalo imagine themselves as having derived from the ground and this sense of place is endemic in Timorese consciousness, for it is from the land that human beings acquire the spiritual vitality that translates into reproductive potency. This fertility derives from the elementals that are thought to house themselves beneath the earth's mantle of soil and rock, and from this abode they venture forth when they are summoned by ritual or human infraction into the material world. From this sacred realm they exercise—if they so choose—their capacities to confer vitality and abundance, thereby enhancing—and even making possible—the daily lives of those who sacrifice to them. From the world of the spirit derive rights in land, whether to reside or to cultivate, for as we have seen mythological charter stipulates that the first human beings who left Mahuma became the owners of the land. By virtue of this temporal precedence they came to exercise political primacy as well.[4]

Tetum-speakers lack an inclusive term embracing all categories of spiritual entity, but they do separate spirits into two broad classes. In a very similar manner to the Nage of Flores (Forth 1998:47–63), one class of spirits, what Gregory Forth calls "free spirits," consists of elementals that are independent of the objects in which they temporarily take up their residence. One of my acquaintances compared spirits of this nature to the wind, making the point that they cannot be defined in terms of the various material manifestations in which they appear. These are the afore-mentioned spiritual "lords of the land" *(rai na'in)* and "lords of the water" *(u'e na'in)*. The second class of spirits consists of *klamar* and *mate bein* (ghosts), which are entities associated very closely with animate things or things that have previously been animate, namely, humans, animals, and plants. The term *klamar* might be thought of as corresponding to the English-language notion of "soul" and provides the stem for a number of compounds, including *klamar-hanoin* (the imagination, mind), *klamar-nia* (intellectual, mental, spiritual), and *klamar-hua* (to nourish the spirit).

Another similarity Tetum spirits share with Nage spirits described by Forth, and one that provides a basis for a general classification of spiritual entities, relates to their place in what might be termed the local "metaphysical geography." *Klamar* are "domesticated" in that although their domicile is the spiritual world they operate within the confines of the human world, whether hamlet, garden, or rice field. "Free spirits," on the other hand, operate in the wilderness, whether adjacent to, or far from, the hamlets, and even when altars are dedicated to them these will be sited within the forest, outside the community of human beings. Ghosts, on the other hand, are identified with the human realm, and their altars are within the houses of their living kin.

Lords of the Land

The term *rai na'in* or "lord of the land," we have already seen, refers to two categories of being. One consists of the aristocratic population of Caraubalo; the other consists of nature spirits. Each enjoys parallel authority and prestige in their respective domains of profane and sacred. Earth spirits dwell in groves of trees, in isolated trees, in cliffs, or at the top of mountains, virtually any natural feature or object that has some abnormality or interesting feature, whether shape, size, or color. Like water spirits, earth spirits are normally invisible but may assume the shape of animals or human beings. Because of the mottled pattern of designs on its body, the reticulated python is identified as a *rai na'in* since this pattern is an index of its otherworldly nature. Other species of snake are not classed as nature spirits, but black cats and beautiful girls are all forms typically assumed by these elementals. For their part, *u'e na'in* or "water spirits" reside in springs, streams, or rivers and assume the form of crocodiles, shrimps, and eels.

Free spirits are domiciled in the underworld, but when they enter the human world they do so at the abnormal or interesting sites mentioned above, which are thus regarded as *lulik* by the populace, and it is at or near these places that they manifest themselves in one form or another to persons who happen to pass by. An encounter with a nature spirit can be lethal, especially in that these spirits are said to have a demonic cast to their nature, and in previous works I have actually referred to them as "demons" (Hicks 1984:5, 92–96). Some Catholic villagers—no doubt under the influence of missionaries—have come to identify them with Satan *(satan)*. Notwithstanding their espousing an alien creed, even Catholics regard nature spirits as being the most powerful *lulik* of all, and everyone to whom I spoke dreaded them and would discuss them only circumspectly, if then. Shamans, who possess many powerful remedies against attacks by any of the other categories of spirit, also view them with the greatest respect and fear their power to impair human life and cause trouble between human beings, as the following tale demonstrates:

> I was told that several years before my arrival, a Mamulak elder, Loi Nahak, was walking to his garden, about three miles from his house, when he found his path barred by a lovely, dark-skinned girl. He had never set eyes on her before. For this reason he feared the girl was a nature spirit, but before Loi could run away, the girl took hold of his hand and invited him to make love. Too stiff with fright to refuse, he lay down in her arms. When he arrived home that evening Dau

Nahak, his wife, sensed all was not well but said nothing. During the night a gigantic female python slid into their bedroom, bewitched Dau into not waking up, and obliged Loi Nahak to copulate with her. With the coming of dawn the python returned to the sacred world. The next day Dau's suspicions made her think of divorce. She and her husband began sleeping in different rooms, and shortly afterwards the marriage broke up.

Both the spirits of the land and the spirits of the water exercise a strong measure of control, for better or worse, over the lives and aspirations of human beings, and individuals who encounter a spirit in the wilderness frequently undergo a miraculous transformation. These transformations provide many folktales, legends, and myths with their main theme describing how, as a result of the encounter, the hero instantly amasses great wealth, acquires enormous physical prowess, becomes invulnerable to death or injury, or enjoys the capability of visiting the world of the spirit and returning. On the other hand, however, nature spirits also can cause infertility, sickness, insanity, and death.

Very occasionally, one hears a narrative that has considerably more institutional importance since it serves as a charter myth, like the story that explains the foundation of the Eel Clan and the establishment of culture as the result of a meeting with a water spirit (Hicks 1984:24–29). The Eel Clan (discussed in chapter 4) is one of the two clans in Mamulak village, and has distinctive properties such as this myth of origin, a set of rights and duties that distinguishes it apart the other clans in the neighborhood, a taboo against killing eels, and an identity defined by the cultural hero (called Ali-iku) who instructed the earliest eel people how to perform their own distinctive rituals and dances and taught them special songs to sing. These early eel people were seven brothers, but the youngest of all, Ali-iku, was really a nature spirit, who, after imparting to his elder brothers these attributes of culture, promptly disappeared into the spirit world.

Men more than women appear to be prone to encounter these entities, perhaps because women are thought to be more closely associated with the earth mother than men and they are considered less likely to be entrapped by the wiles of these spirits. Another possible reason women are less commonly featured in tales of this sort is because storytelling is a masculine art form. Still, as in Loi Nahak's adventure, not all tales about spirits are formal narratives, nor are nature spirits invariably given a female identity, as this tale shows:

The wife's father (a Catholic, I might remark) of a neighbor of mine in Viqueque town was out hunting in the forest one day with several other men, and because he grew tired his companions left him to rest by himself. While he was resting he saw two black soldiers in uniform approaching. They noticed him lying there and started discussing what to do with him. The black soldier to the man's right wanted to seize him and shoot him. The one on the left preferred to leave him alone. The man trembled but could not speak. The soldiers eventually decided to leave him alone, and vanished into thin air. The man knew there were no military encampments in the area, and that African soldiers would not be resident in Timor. He concluded therefore that they were land spirits. For three weeks he could not bring himself to tell anyone about his adventure, a reticence probably resulting from the belief that such spirits dislike being spoken about and may punish the person who reveals the encounter. In general one finds that Timorese prefer to have companions when they travel in the countryside, since spirits tend to manifest themselves only to unaccompanied individuals.

Another narrative has as its theme the authority spirits have to confer fecundity and abundance.

A man, so the story goes, was cultivating his garden, which happened to be located a long way from his house. A well-dressed woman suddenly presented herself before him. The farmer was surprised because there were no houses nearby. The woman asked him to marry her, but the man replied, "I have a wife at home." He was too frightened to keep refusing her importuning, however, so after saying that he would sleep with his human wife during one part of the day and the spirit wife during the other part, he married her. In return, she gave him anything he asked for—buffaloes, horses, and houses. His human wife never discovered he had a spirit wife.

The appearance of a nature spirit masquerading in female form is almost invariably that of an attractive Timorese woman, whereas in male form its appearance is typically marked by some unusual quality, for example, an African soldier where none might be expected or by some type of odd behavior, as we find in the next narrative:

One Caraubalo man of the Eel Clan related to me that his father had once seen a naked old man playing childlike with water in a stream—something prohibited to members of this clan by their origin myth. His skin was extremely red and his hair was white. Like a simpleton might, he waved at his man, moving only the palm and fingers of his hand, and with his elbow and wrist stiff. My interlocutor's father called out "*hoi! hoi!*" admonishing the old man to stop behaving like a child; but the old man just waved back in the same way and kept on playing. Later, a member of the father's clan dreamed the old man had been asking for a young boy from their group to be sacrificed to him, and he concluded from this that he had seen a *rai na'in*.

Nature spirits are fond of taking up residence in geodes, stones with a typically spherical shape found all over Timor and having a hollow cavity

filled with crystals. They come in varying sizes. A geode identified as the
abode of a particular spirit is termed a *foho matan* (stone + eye). Sometimes the *foho matan* forms part of an altar dedicated to the spirit and may
rest directly on the ground. Sometimes, as in the altar of the Eel clan
(Hicks 1984:74–76), it sits on a flat stone slab that is placed directly on the
ground, or it might sit on a flat base, varying in thickness from eighteen
inches to six feet, made up of many smaller stones. (See plate 4.) This
kind of altar reflects the gender duality characteristic of Tetum symbolism. Whereas the geode itself is considered female, as is implied by the
designation *fatuk kabua* (pregnant stone), the flat base on which it rests is
regarded as its male partner, the *fatuk bein* (the big stone) or *fatuk messa*
(the table stone).

The attitude in Caraubalo regarding these geodes is on a par with that
of the Northern Tetum, among whom Grijzen (1904:75) reports that a
man who finds a geode in the wilderness expects sometime later to have a
dream in which he receives a visit from a nature spirit who encourages
him to establish a relationship with it, and in exchange for the sacrifice of
a chicken or young pig, it offers something highly desirable, usually
wealth or power. The spirit also tells the man where in the wilderness he
must relocate the stone, a place that will now be its earthly home. If the
spirit demands the sacrifice of a young animal, a death in the dreamer's
family is presaged so that on waking, the finder of the stone will consult a
trusted shaman for help in breaking whatever covenant he may have
agreed to during the dream (Grijzen 1904:75). The price of reneging on
this agreement may involve sacrificing an adult pig, which apparently is
valuable enough to deflect any resentment the *rai na'in* may feel by the
man's breach of promise. Should the man be satisfied with the arrange-
ment, however, he becomes the stone's owner, and the nature spirit
becomes his guardian and that of the stone.

The morning following his dream the man goes to the general area
that the *rai na'in* has specified for locating the stone. There he offers the
sacrifice stipulated by the spirit together with some betel-chew[5] (*buran*
or "blood of the areca"), which is of varying shades of red in color, and
invariably accompanies any ritual contact with a spirit. He then returns
home to seek shamanic advice about where precisely to situate the
geode. For a land spirit the best place is usually said to be near some
sizeable rock or large tree, like a banyan tree, whereas a water spirit
might favor a place where two watercourses converge, or near a spring,
or along a riverbank. The chosen site is now considered *rai lulik* or
"sacred ground," the same term used, it will be recalled, for the sacred
world, and henceforth regarded as tabooed for cultivation.

Neither can any trees in the immediate locality be cut down nor can
wood be gathered to kindle fires, while the only animals that may be

slain in the now-sacred area are those that are to be sacrificed to the spirit. Springs flowing nearby cannot be contaminated by washing or urination. These taboos are not restricted to the kinship group of the man who guards the geode; they must be observed by all residents of the local community.

The owner builds an altar, sets the stone down on it, and inserts a stick in the ground nearby. From this stick some material commemoration of the sacrifices made to the guardian of the stone will be hung, perhaps the shell of a coconut whose contents served as an aspersion for the spirit or the jawbone of a pig whose flesh was sacrificed. On special occasions blood may also be sacrificed to the stone.

Henceforth, in exchange for regular sacrifices of meat and rice offered at dawn—one of the four periods of transition during the day (the others are midday, sunset, and midnight)—the spirit provides benefits to the owner of the stone, his family, and his clan. These include fertility, health, and an abundance of other good things. Delinquency in making these sacrifices or offering gifts the spirit considers inadequate, on the other hand, induces infertility, sickness, and death for family, crops, and livestock (Grijzen 1904:76). When such misfortunes occur the miscreant consults his shaman, who performs an augury ritual to identify the precise cause and determine the appropriate expiatory sacrifice to make. The sacrifice will invariably incorporate seven betel leaves and seven areca nuts from which betel-chew can be made. The number seven and betel-chew have special claims on the Timorese imagination, as they have on other populations throughout the archipelago. Both are constantly resorted to in rituals and appear throughout oral literatures, where they evoke the sense of abundance, life, and fertility. We find, accordingly, that the most common sacrificial offerings are of various shades of red—red pigs and red buffaloes in particular as well as the ubiquitous red betel-chew.

The anecdotes describing the circumstances in which men find geodes are many, though I have never heard a tale where the finder was female. These stories can highlight the tenacity that underlies indigenous convictions regarding beliefs in these spirits and demonstrates their strength even among persons under the influence of Christianity, as we find in the following story:

> One villager told me that the day following his discovery of a red stone, a local man noticed that the stone had given birth to a tiny red stone. This baby stone lay beside its mother, and he wanted nothing to do with either stone. So he dug a hole in the ground, poured holy water (water blessed by a Catholic priest) on the stones, placed them inside the hole, and covered them up with soil. My interlocutor included the remark that the mother and her baby would simply have

appeared again had he not used the blessed water, which ensured
they would not return.

Rai na'in can also be allied with social groups of various kinds for,
as in the case of the Eel clan, nature spirits also play the role of cultural
heroes, and as such serve as the founders of descent groups. The Eel
shrine in Mamulak is dedicated to the water spirit that founded the Eel
clan, and the three geodes it possesses house the spirit of its cultural
hero (Hicks 1984:75). In the past, *liurais* among the Northern Tetum
owned what might be termed "stones of state" (Grijzen 1904:75)
whose *rai na'in* exercised dominion over the entire kingdom and their
descent groups. Members of these descent groups were called "sons of
the earth people" *(ema rai oan)* and were responsible for performing sacrificial rituals to the spirits.

Not all geodes are invested with the power of *lulik*, however, and even
those that are do not invariably wish to establish a relationship with the
human beings who pick them up. According to one villager, "If I take
home a stone that is *lulik*, when I dream that night the spirit comes to me
and says: 'My name is Miguel [or whatever name it claims to have]. I am
a *lulik* stone. You must put me back!' In the morning when I awake I
return the stone to its original place."

The Soul

The term *klamar* is used for spiritual entities that inhabit the material
shape of both nonhuman and human entities. Apart from the deer, the
nonhuman entities are all domesticated. They are the buffalo soul *(karau
klamar)*, the corn soul *(batar klamar)*, and the rice soul *(hare klamar)*, whose
functions are limited to conferring or withholding fecundity from the
human population. The living human being is thought of as a composite
structure consisting of a material aspect, the body *(lolon)*, and the soul
(klamar moris), which is thought to reside inside the head. In this respect
an individual mirrors the opposition between the profane world and the
sacred world.

An individual's life *(moris)* begins when the soul assumes residence in
his or her body, and although villagers were not at all clear about when this
might occur, I have the impression this takes place during gestation. Nor is
it apparent from where the soul originates, if it in fact originates from anywhere, but once installed this sacred dimension of the individual remains
closely allied to his or her physical aspect. Life depends on this connection,
and death *(mate)* is attributed to the permanent loss of the soul. The soul of
a dead person is termed the *mate klamar* and is thought to be immortal.

Wrenched from its body at death, for twelve months after the corpse
has been interred the dead soul, envious that its kin are still living, flits
back and forth between the two worlds, plaguing the hamlet of its erst-

while kin, causing illness and sometimes death. A final rite (*keta mate* [*keta* = to separate, to divide; *mate* = dead]) is needed to dispatch it finally to the sacred world, where it joins the ancestors and becomes an ancestor itself. Until this rite is performed, the dead soul is only an occasional visitor to the sacred world, unlike nature spirits and ghosts, whose permanent domicile is the sacred world, and who enter the material world only for specific purposes, usually in response to ritual evocations, misconduct by human beings, or a desire to find some human acolyte to supply it with sacrifices.

Witches

A witch *(buan)* is not a spiritual entity in the same sense as nature spirits and the soul, for it partakes of both spiritual and material natures. The witch lacks any benevolent attributes whatsoever, and is an incorrigibly malevolent quasi-human being who lives like an otherwise legitimate resident within the community of the hamlet but also is a frequenter of the forest wilderness. People are extremely vague as to witches' properties and profess to be ignorant as to the exact way in which they go about their nefarious activities. Indeed, persons with whom I raised the question of witches gave me the impression they were concerned that even discussing witches might incur retribution from these dangerous creatures.

What they did say is that witches are nocturnal and endowed with the capacity to transform themselves from their human shape into that of a dark bird of the night, most commonly an owl, or a small bird of a restless disposition they call the *berliku*.[6] This is not to say that all owls are thought of as witches. Only black owls are so regarded, but the cry of any owl at night is thought to signify the death of a member of the community. Owls may be killed, but it is *lulik* to eat them or, for that matter, the *berliku*, whose association with evil is difficult to account for. The nocturnal nature of the owl, of course, might be thought to evoke images of dread, though another creature of the night, the bat, evokes no such dire feeling, and its flesh can be consumed.

At times witches may present themselves as black dwarfs, and at other times they fly through the darkness where they can be detected by the red light they emit (cf. Needham 1978:41). In their human guise they may betray their propensity for witchcraft by possessing a character perceived by their neighbors as morally dubious or by otherwise behaving unsociably, but (at least to my knowledge during my stay in Viqueque) such individuals were never directly accused of witchcraft or openly anathematized.

One strategy for mischief, which people say characterizes a witch, involves creeping stealthily into a house when the inhabitants are asleep and seizing the throat of a particular sleeper singled out as a victim. Bendita, a servant girl my wife and I employed, described how one night a witch jumped on her back when she was sleeping and grasped her throat.

Instantly she woke up and uttered a loud cry that frightened off the assail-
ant. Owing to the penchant people say witches have for entering apertures
such as doors, windows, and mouths, before retiring a person who suspects
he or she might become a victim that night will sprinkle some salt (an anti-
dote against witchcraft) around the doors and windows of the house and
rub salt on their lips. I was told that witches could enter dreams to entice the
sleeper into making a lethal medicine with which to poison a kinsperson.

Unlike dead souls, which are troublesome for no more than a year or
so after a person's death, witches offer a perpetual threat to life, health,
and fertility, and so they arouse more constant trepidation than spirits.
Furthermore, in contrast with nature spirits, a mutually beneficial relationship can never be established between a human being and a witch,
nor can a witch be induced by a sacrificial offering to release a victim it
has selected to persecute. Despite the abhorrence in which they are held,
buans are not regarded as powerful as *rai na'ins* or *mate beins* because they
are partly human and so do not command the unrestrained capacity for
action that these entities enjoy.

The Sacred Queen

The *liurai feto lulik*, "sacred queen," who was one of the protagonists
in the myth that described the emergence of Timor, is known today only
in myths, one of which vaguely links her with Bibilutu, an ancient kingdom formerly located between Viqueque town and the sea. Another myth
associates her with the origin of fire, which is an alternative version to
another myth describing the origin of fire (Hicks 1984:95), and it introduces a ritual figure known as the rainmaker *(liurai lulik)*:

> At one time, according to the narrative, people did not know about
> fire and would eat their meat raw, preparing it only by beating it with
> a buffalo horn. When the meat had been beaten until it was white in
> color they would mix it with blood and consume it. The local rain-
> maker, whose name was Rubi Koko La Koto, was the husband of
> Cassa Sonek (one of the three founders of Caraubalo identified previ-
> ously) who was a sacred queen living at the Mahuma vent. Cassa
> Sonek knew about fire, though, and when she married the rainmaker
> she brought this knowledge with her. Rubi Koko La Koto owned two
> dogs whose names were Bui Adi and Lai Adi, and one day they
> caught and killed a pig. The queen had the meat cooked on a sacred
> hearth *(lalian lulik)* and the rainmaker ate the first meat ever cooked
> for an ordinary mortal.

The Priest

The term *makair lulik* or *dato lulik* denotes a ritual functionary I refer
to as "priest."[7] The priest is an office-holder who usually inherits his posi-

tion from a male in the paternal line and carries out public sacrifices on behalf of the *suku* community as a whole. Household rituals, by contrast, are private rites generally performed by the wife, or, if they involve a descent group, by the wife of a prominent elder. The priest also serves as guardian of any ritual house *(uma lulik)* that the *suku* or descent group may own. By the time of my research in Caraubalo, missionary activity had brought about the abandonment or destruction of most of these secred houses.

A priest traditionally exercised an important political duty during the wars that occurred between kingdoms before the Portuguese pacification. At the ritual house owned by the *suku* he would administer a blessing to the warriors prior to their departure on a raid. The ritual, called *kuta*, involved his chewing betel and daubing the betel-chew on the warriors' foreheads. When the betel-chew was completely dry the priest would examine the stains to determine its shade of red. A stain that he judged to be a clear red hue was auspicious, but one that he saw as "black" *(metan)* meant its wearer would be likely to be killed. In the latter case the priest would encourage the man to remain home. Occasionally, if the priest were indisposed, a local shaman would act in his stead. However, since a shaman was only substituting for the priest, whose office symbolized the priest's descent group, the shaman lacked the authority to perform the ritual at the community's ritual house, and would perform the ritual at any convenient location.

Another figure involved in war rituals was the rainmaker. One of the rainmaker's functions was to accompany the warriors to the vicinity of the enemy where he would then extract lime from his sacred lime container, and with the white powder in the palm of his left hand, he would blow it in the general direction where the enemy troops were thought to lurk, thereby rendering his own warriors invisible.

The Shaman

The Timorese shaman is the local version of a magico-religious functionary known throughout much of the eastern archipelago as the *dukun*, whose position, unlike that of priest, is not inherited nor is it an office in the sense that it has an existence independent of its incumbent. A *suku* may have any number of shamans, or it may have none if there is no one of sufficient reputation or talent to undertake shamanic challenges. In Caraubalo I was acquainted personally with two shamans: Mateus, a twenty-five-year-old man from Bua Laran, and Claudina, a woman who may have been from the Ina-Aman lineage of Kia Mahan.

Timorese shamans are ritual specialists credited with the capacity to see "far" *(do'ok)* into the future or portend the meaning of current events whose significance is unclear to most people—hence, the term by which they are known, *matan do'ok* (*matan* = eye). This talent for prognostication and the capacity to analyze problematic situations with some degree of shrewdness, combined with an esoteric knowledge of medicines, comprise the defining features of this ritual practitioner. Elaborating for my benefit his description of shamanistic devices, one villager, perhaps a trifle histrionically, held a betel leaf over his right eye and told me that a shaman would be able to see right through its green opacity. Among the most common problems a shaman is called on to solve is determining the human or spiritual source of his or her client's ill health.

Like the witch, the shaman transcends both the profane world and the sacred domain, but in contrast to the rainmaker and priest, the shaman's power does not derive from succeeding in patrilineal succession from his or her father, but rather through allegedly commanding this talent for prediction and interpretation—"farsightedness"—and having the capability to convince clients he or she has either cured them or appreciably ameliorated their ills. Some persons become shamans after an encounter in the wilderness with a nature spirit, and in such a case it is this elemental that becomes the shaman's mentor and instructs the human acolyte in the arcane intelligence necessary for success in this profession. A few successes with clients and a shaman will gradually amass a clientele.

A shaman's repertoire of tools includes betel-chew, which he or she daubs on client's body in order to discern the facts appropriate for a responsible assessment of the case. Betel-chew provides the practitioner with the means of transcending the boundary separating the secular from the sacred and where necessary communing with the spirits. Thus armed with insight from both worlds the shaman is then able to discern what is going on and decide the appropriate cure. Another technique for gaining information is for the shaman to scrutinize the color patterns on the outside shell of a hen's egg.

Payments to the shaman are required since material reward is an integral component of the ritual relationship established between the shaman and his or her client. A parallel exists here with the relationship between human beings and spirits since reciprocity between both parties is an essential component for success. Gift giving symbolizes this pact of reciprocity, and failure to comply with this express provision vitiates the integrity of the relationship. The consequences may be calamitous, as Rubi Loik, resident of Cailulik hamlet and one of my most willing informants, made clear to me in the following recollection. His anecdote also shows that some shamans are believed to possess the power to raise the dead, a personal example of the resurrection, a theme frequently encountered in Timorese myths and folktales.

> One day, as Rubi Loik's mother's brother lay dying he was visited
> by three shamans who examined him, uttered words in a strange

language, and left. They returned shortly, and discovering the man had died, they stood to the left of the corpse, hoisted his stiff body onto its feet, and laid him down on the ground. One shaman then took a machete, placed the end of the handle against his own lips and with the point towards the corpse blew down its length. This action of breathing imparted life into the corpse, which got up. The resurrected man then went in search of a buffalo with which to pay the shaman. Although he searched everywhere, he was unable find one. His failure had a lethal effect because, since they were not given their payment, two of the shamans died in succession, followed by Rubi Loik's uncle, and then by the third shaman.

Shamans take advantage of a variety of medicines *(ai moruk)* in their work, and they can be regarded as the medicine specialists of Timorese society, even though they are not the exclusive owners of this intelligence. Any person who knows the right medicine can use it, and knowledge of this kind forms part of the general knowledge of every villager. Of all generic remedies, the most popular is betel-chew, though is not usually classed as *ai moruk*, and unlike *ai moruk* is invested with a heavy symbolic load. A common prophylactic that is thought to act as a generic protector against all manner of harm is twenty or so dry seeds of a plant I was unable to identify wrapped up in a small piece of paper. Another medicine, called *manu makikik*, which is the denotation for a species of predator known as the brahminy kite *(Haliastur indus)*, consists of a small piece of bone dangling on a string around the wearer's neck. From this bone extends a cord at the end of which is a thin needle-shaped piece of bone. This amulet is said to be a protection against witches. To defend young chickens from avian raptors, a man will erect adjacent to his house a structure consisting of a ten-foot bamboo pole from which dangles a cord. Attached to the cord at the top is the root of a plant called the *busa oan*, below which dangles a broken fragment of a cooking pot. This ensemble functions empirically as a scarecrow but, people believe its power to deter raptors is of a magical order.

While these medicines are beneficial, I was able to identify several medicines that inflict harm. They include a white powder that a malcontent may place between his first finger and thumb and cast with lethal intentions in the direction of his or her intended victim. People told me that a certain harmful powder, if deposited on footprints or on the remains of an intended victim's cigarette, also has lethal authority.

Endnotes

[1] I thank Gérard Francillon for pointing out to me this use of the term *sau*.
[2] The concept appears elsewhere in Timor as, for example, among the Atoni of West Timor who have the term *le'u* (Schulte Nordholt 1971:147). Schulte Nordholt, however,

does not regard the term as corresponding to *luli* since he (in my opinion incorrectly) regards the Tetum term *luli* as equivalent only to the Atoni term *nuni* or "taboo" and not embracing the two concepts of "taboo" and "sacred."

[3] I shall only summarize its relevant essentials here. For the full version, see *A Maternal Religion* (Hicks 1984, 1–2).

[4] More than three decades later, in another part of East Timor, I heard an elder who was, or at least had been, a politically active man, attribute the failure of the Indonesian administration to govern *sukus* successfully to the fact that they would select as leaders of the *suku* men who did not command popular respect. Although they occupied, in effect, the office of *liurai* they were not of *liurai* descent, because *liurais* cannot be "made." As my friend put it, "*liurais* need to be dug for," a figure of speech that makes a telling link between the office and the land.

[5] One indulgence the people of Timor share with many other Asian folk is betel-chewing, about which they are as compulsive as tobacco-smoking Westerners. A leaf from a betel tree is sprinkled with powdered lime. The leaf is twisted tightly to prevent the powder from filtering out, and together with one or two slices of areca nut, is stuffed into the mouth. A minute's chewing produces a spittle (areca blood) ranging in color from bright scarlet to brown. Mildly narcotic, this mixture is pleasant enough once the neophyte has learned how to clear his throat without spitting the red, frothy mass down his shirt, where the stains set stubbornly. Betel-chewing is an essential component of most Tetum rituals.

[6] The word *berliku*, when used as a verb, means "to bob" or "to dart around."

[7] In some Tetum areas this figure is called *makdean* or *nai lulik*.

Chapter 3

The Land and Its People

The natural environment of Caraubalo evokes the concept of *lulik* in many of its features. The source of spiritual authority lies within the earth, but the spiritual dimensions of Tetum experience are more than merely locational. The soil is thought of as material to be fertilized by the semen of the father god whose power of fecundity descends from the clouds as rain. The children of the earth mother traditionally claim to control the natural resources of the land by virtue of leaving her womb before other human beings did, and every season multitudes of ritual performances reconnect the land with the spiritual forces underlying it. Nor do these sacred forces remain in this nether location. For the most part, the spirits exert an influence over human existence only when they enter the physical world formed by the human and natural landscapes of Caraubalo, and to understand in the fullest sense how the Tetum eke out a living in their unpredictable environment we need to have some acquaintance with the sacred powers they attribute to the environment.

The Layout

Timor, which is about three hundred miles long, has a mountainous backbone rising to eight thousand feet, flanked by northern and southern coastlines that in East Timor display contrasting landscapes. The northern coast, which abuts the "feminine sea" (so-called because it is relatively calm), ends in most places in swamps or enters the sea in cliffs. The southern coast, which abuts the "masculine sea" (a violent stretch of water), consists of an undulating plain extending inland. Caraubalo's transitional character is directly reflected in the local ecology for the *suku* (figure 3) lies where the plain merges into the uplands rising gradually into what Joachim Metzner (1977:33) calls the "Southern Foothill Zone" to meet the more precipitous landscape of the central mountains.

Another natural factor influencing ecology is the climatic cycle. Little annual variation in temperature occurs, which means that the climatic cycle is in fact the rainfall cycle with two wet seasons (November–January and March–June) and two dry seasons (February and July–October) that help determine the Tetum seasonal cycle of economic, kinship, and ritual activities, which figure 4 summarizes. In areas where soil conditions and relief are favorable, the heavy rainfall coupled with the consistently high temperatures (80 to 90 degrees F) have produced dense stands of tropical forest containing such species as teak, casuarina, mahogany, palm trees, sago, and ironwood. Lower down or where the soil is poorer, savanna replaces forest, stretching in some localities for many miles. Being in a zone of topographic and ecological transition, Caraubalo has a mixture of forest and savanna.

The region surrounding Viqueque town, the administrative capital of Viqueque district, is dominated by the River Cuha, which flows down from the central massif of Timor through the town of Ossú to enter the sea 12 miles south of Caraubalo at a place called Beaçu. From Ossú the 300-foot contour follows the river on its way down the 12 miles to Viqueque town, which is about 150 feet above sea level. Just on the outskirts of the town, a belt of hard rock, which is part of southernmost rim of the Southern Foothill Zone, pushes the river abruptly eastward from its general north–south trend before it enters the settlement and then several hundred yards further on encounters a second band of hard rock that forces it to veer westward. Inside the loop thus defined the town of Viqueque has grown up, and with 300-foot hills to the east and some high ground to the west it stands in a natural basin less than 300 feet above sea level, with flatter ground within which are located six of the seven villages of Caraubalo, the single exception being Sira Lari, which lies several miles to the north in the Southern Foothill Zone.

The six villages, which are all Tetum-speaking (in contrast to that of Sira Lari, which is inhabited by speakers of Makassai), are generally about 150 feet above sea level.[1] Here, on the gently undulating flood plain of the River Cuha, and on the flat stretches of land that finger their way between ridges jutting down from the Southern Foothill Zone, are the most fertile soils in the region. Gardens and groves of coconut trees thrive so well here that this locality, according to Metzner, has one of the highest population densities in all of East Timor, the ridges themselves being too steep for either residence or cultivation.

	November	December	January	February	March	April	May	June	July	August	September	October
Months (fulan)	—	—	—	bibi	kakosek	basuk	kailor	datalor	dau aman	luru kama	—	—
Climate	WET	WET	WET	DRY	WET	WET	WET	WET	WET	DRY	DRY	DRY
Seasons	rai udan	rai udan	rai udan	ua'i loro kik	rai udan	rai udan	rai udan	rai udan	rai udan	ua'i loro	ua'i loro	ua'i loro
Horticulture	corn planted; most other crops planted	other crops harvested as necessary		corn harvested	rice planted	rice planted; corn planted; most other crops planted	corn planted	most other crops harvested	most other crops harvested	corn harvested; rice harvested; areca harvested	corn harvested	
	weeding	weeding	weeding		weeding	weeding	weeding; bird scaring	weeding; bird scaring		garden fired	garden fired	garden dug and fired
Household location	garden	mainly hamlet	mainly hamlet	garden	garden	mainly garden	mainly hamlet	mainly garden	hamlet	hamlets and gardens	hamlets and gardens	mainly garden
Social activities	a few marriages	making cloth and implements; some visiting		no visiting	little visiting		much visiting	much visiting	much visiting	marriages; housebuilding	marriages; housebuilding	housebuilding; some visiting

Figure 4.   The Ideal Seasonal Cycle in Caraubalo

Like the hamlets, the majority of gardens are located on the western bank of the River Cuha, where the more fertile soils, particularly those on the alluvial flats immediately west of the River Cuha, can be cultivated for more successive years as semipermanent gardens, and these are owned by Mane Hat and Mamulak. The marl soils on the eastern side impair the effectiveness of the drainage, which, suggests Metzner (1977:59), probably renders them less fertile. In the wet season they become extremely plastic and sticky and in the dry season they are rutted and bone-hard, and villagers cultivate few gardens here.

Tetum villagers in Caraubalo are not only advantageously placed in that they can cultivate the best soils in the area, but because of the elevation of their habitat they are not as vulnerable to malaria, the most devastating source of ill-health in East Timor, as they would be were they to occupy the plain itself as do other Tetum-speaking populations. Metzner (1977:239) contends that "Malaria . . . plays a decisive role in the island ecosystem," and adds that extensive tracts of otherwise cultivable land remain unexploited on the plains because the Timorese fear contracting this disease. In Caraubalo, he points out, the incidence rate of 11–50 percent for malaria, though high, is lower than on the plains. I can testify to the fact that Timorese are well aware of the correlation between altitude and incidence of malaria, and Ossú's cool temperatures and absence of malaria are envied. With its transitional location, Caraubalo has better soils than the uplands and less malaria than the lowlands, a beneficial conjunction that contributes to the fact that of all the ten *sukus* in the home subdistrict, Caraubalo has by far the densest population.[2]

Unlike the well-dispersed settlements in the Southern Foothill Zone itself and in the mountains, these basin settlements are so concentrated that communications are easy in the dry season, and the proximity of Viqueque town provides Tetum-speaking villagers with greater employment opportunities than the Makassai. Social change, therefore, has thus been more accelerated here than in Sira Lari and the other villages in the uplands.

A hamlet strikes the observer as a complex of up to about half a dozen houses *(uma)* that are typically raised on wooden piles about a yard above the ground. The houses are arranged in no particular order around a central plaza, which in the dry season, like the bridle paths, is bone-hard. These settlements are located near convenient sources of water supply—springs, streams, or the River Cuha itself. The hamlets comprising the villages in Caraubalo are for the most part scattered about the savanna and woodland, and some Mamulak hamlets intermingle with those of Mane Hat (figure 5). The hamlets of Mamulak and the village of Cabira Oan spread across both banks of this river, though most of the hamlets lie on the west bank. The hamlets making up Lamaclaran, Vessa, and Has Abut, however, lie on the east bank.

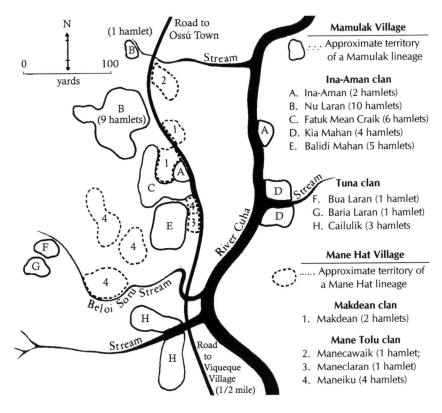

Figure 5.   Mamulak and Mane Hat Hamlets

Land Ownership

Land in Caraubalo is jointly owned by the two aristocratic *(rai na'in)* villages, Mamulak and Mane Hat. Residents of the other five villages, strictly speaking, have only the status of tenants *(ema rai)* with rights of usufruct. At any rate, this is what one is told by the residents of Mamulak and Mane Hat, but the notion of land ownership is more vague than this forthright claim would suggest. In practice anyone may build a garden just about anywhere in his own *suku*, but a garden is allowed to lie fallow after several years' cultivation, and if the owner has made clear his intention of returning to continue cultivating it (e.g., by collecting the fruits from such trees as coconut, areca, and banana that may grow in the garden), no one will take it over without his consent. Land in other *sukus* may be cultivated as long as permission is obtained from the local equiva-

lents of the *makair fukun/dato ua'in* and *liurai*. One consequence of the
scarcity of good, available, arable land is that many gardens cultivated by
residents of Mamulak and Mane Hat are located in Luca *suku*, several
hours' trudge from Caraubalo.

The aristocrats justify their claims to ownership of the *suku* by
recourse to the myth of Mahuma, which as we have seen portrays them as
descendants of Rubi Rika, Lera Tiluk, and Cassa Sonek who were the
first human beings to be born from the ground. The rest of the autochthonous Caraubalo population is made up of persons of commoner rank
(*ema rai* or "people of the land") who are, as noted earlier, their tenants in
virtue of the fact that they are said to descend from ancestors who followed this trio out of the Mahuma vent. These autochthones, whether
aristocratic landlords or commoners, are referred to as *ema dakan* or "the
people of the *dakan* plant," because it was by means of this plant that their
ancestors were able to clamber out. *Dakan* has certain totemic associations for such people, it being *lulik* for them to chew it.

The *suku* has two other categories of resident. One, of course, consists
of Makassai commoners who immigrated into Caraubalo in recent years
and founded the village of Sira Lari. The other consists of the descendants of Tetum aristocrats who came into the *suku* in mythological times:
members of the Makdean clan, in Mane Hat village, and the Tuna clan,
in Mamulak village. The arrival of the newcomers is registered in myths
that describe the leaders of the immigrants asking and receiving permission from the landowners to settle in the *suku*. Because they were immigrants they were granted land with less fertile soil than that of their
landlords, and although they are recognized as aristocrats they are not
regarded as exemplary *rai na'in* because they are not autochthonous like
the aristocratic members of Ina-Aman clan and Mane Tolu clan, or even
like the members of the commoner clans in the other Tetum villages in
the *suku*. Depending upon which version of the myth is recited, permission for them to settle in Caraubalo is described as having been granted
either by the *dato ua'in*, *makair fukun*, or *liurai*. In the following myth we
learn that it was the *liurai* of that time, a figure called by the composite
name, "Rubi Rika Lera Tiluk" [*sic*], who is credited with giving permission to the first Tuna people to settle in Mamulak.

> The myth tells how Lela Sou, eldest brother of a group of seven broth-
> ers who were the first members of the Eel clan, arrived in Caraubalo
> hoping to meet the *liurai* of Caraubalo who was called Rubi Rika Lera
> Tiluk[3] in the land that was at the time called Beloi, but which is
> known today as Beloi Soru. It was here that these two talked. The *liu-
> rai* showed Lela Sou four pieces of land, promising to give Lela Sou
> one as a gift on which to settle down. Lela Sou selected one of them,
> took possession of the land, and settled down with his belongings.

Land Use

Timorese in Caraubalo are overwhelmingly subsistence cultivators, though raising animals is also important. Men hunt deer, monkeys, and birds, but for sport rather than food. Fishing and netting prawns is more important, and foraging for wild fruits, nuts, and berries by women and younger unmarried men becomes a life-sustaining activity in years when the rains have failed and starvation is a threat. Prominent among the natural resources is the Arenga palm *(Arenga saccharifera)*, whose bounty includes palm wine, coffins, ropes, thatching material for house roofs, and bungs for the tubes of bamboo in which the palm wine is carried. Bamboo is used for a wide variety of products, and other plants, bushes, and trees are sources for medicines *(ai moruk)*, glue, and oil to light lamps.

Tetum existence, however, depends most of all on the products of the allotment *(kintal)* and the garden *(to'os)*. Scholarly opinion differs on the question of whether the Timorese were cultivating corn and rice when the Portuguese arrived on the island or whether they grew root crops as their staple crops, especially taro. By the year 1700, however, corn had definitely become the staple crop, and so it remains today. Dry rice is also very important and is usually cultivated with corn and root crops, where the soil is more fertile and weeds less of a problem. It tends to be cultivated on land that has recently been claimed from the forest, and involves more weeding and requires more work as well as needing more moisture evenly distributed over the vegetative period of the year (Metzner 1977:124).

Wet rice, which the Tetum think of as being inferior in taste to dry rice, is grown in flat fields or hilly terraces. In striking contrast to the Makassai area north of the Cuha Basin, the cultivation of wet rice is rare in Caraubalo. Of the two wet rice fields owned by inhabitants of its six Tetum-speaking villages, one belongs to the *suku* chief, João da Sá Viana, and the other belongs to the Tuna clan. These exceptions result from two special circumstances. As *suku* chief, João da Sá Viana enjoys the legal entitlement of having an unpaid labor force of up to one hundred Caraubalo villagers work on his fields, and as a clan with a tradition of affinal links with Makassai descent groups, Tuna agnates have adopted this feature of local Makassai culture.

The most important root crops are yams, taro, sweet potatoes, and cassava, which require less weeding than corn or rice. Their sowing and harvesting limits are also less restrictive, and rather than storing them Caraubalo families harvest them as needed. Families supplement their diet with peanuts, cowpeas, French beans, and other vegetables, fruits, and herbs the Portuguese introduced, like pumpkins and onions.

The characteristic style of cultivation throughout Timor is slash-and-burn, a technique that varies slightly according to whether the farmer is making a new garden (or retaking one that he has allowed to lie fallow for several years) or whether he is just continuing to cultivate the same garden as in the previous year. If the garden is new or being reclaimed, then sometime during the dry season he hacks away at the tangle of undergrowth with his machete to clear away as much vegetation as the simple tool permits. He then sets the rubble on fire. After the ashes are sufficiently cool to permit work, the soil is prepared for planting. If the farmer is merely continuing to cultivate the same garden, he allows the damp weeds that have accumulated over the wet growing season to dry for one or two months during the dry season. Then, in about October, he burns them, a process of clearing away the undergrowth known as *rai leren* or *lere rai* (to clear the land). Every year this clearing of the undergrowth and burning of the weeds that have accumulated over the year is repeated before the soil can be prepared. When, after a few years, the fertilizing power of the ashes wanes and weeds become too intractable to eliminate, the household abandons its garden, which reverts to a tough grass called *Imperata cylindrica* and becomes overgrown by bushes. The farmer allows the former garden to lie fallow for several years to allow sufficient fertility to return to the soil before clearing it the next time.

Once the undergrowth has been cleared away and the weeds reduced to ash, the farmer then enters the next stage in the preparation of the soil. Depending on the local terrain, his personal circumstances, and his inclination, he can follow one of two courses. One consists of requesting help from his kin and household to assist him. In this process, which goes by the terms *so'a rai* or *fila rai* (to turn over the soil; to till), about a half dozen men and women, all facing the same direction and each holding a digging stick in either hand, turn over the soil in unison. This technique, though consuming much more time than the common method described below and requiring cooperation between the workers, produces a much greater crop yield because this technique makes longer periods under cultivation possible. This method retains soil moisture during dry spells more effectively, encourages rainwater to enter the soil more easily, and discourages the growth of weeds (which are detrimental to the storage of soil moisture) during the nonvegetative period (Metzner 1977:122–123). Because of the amount of labor involved with *so'a rai* Metzner suggests that its use in a particular area implies overpopulation. Once the soil has been tilled the farmer digs holes in the ground with a short digging stick made from the casuarina tree and plants the seeds. *So'a rai* is carried out only every other year after the garden has first been cultivated, but after several years, the soil's declining fertility requires that it be resorted to every year. The fertility of its alluvial soils makes *so'a rai* cultivation prominent on the River

Cuha flood plain in Caraubalo, where rotation cycles of 3–5 years' cultivation followed by 5–10 years' fallow are frequent (Metzner 1977:175).

The more common method, which, unlike *so'a rai*, is possible on soils that are shallow, sandy, or stony, is for the farmer to eschew tilling and just dig holes and insert the seeds, a method requiring the least work, of course, and allowing a single worker to prepare a garden quickly. Gardens that are freshly cut from the wilderness are usually seeded according to this method, at least for a few years to allow the roots from the original plants to rot away before *so'a rai* becomes practicable. This method is the most popular with the Timorese because it can be practiced on steep slopes and takes less time, which is an important factor when the arrival of the rains catches a household by surprise.

The Caraubalo Tetum grow their crops in two kinds of plots. One is a small allotment, the aforementioned *kintal,* near or adjacent to the household's residence, in which is grown a variety of produce that includes breadfruits, jackfruits, mangos, papayas, and coconut trees. Under these trees grow bananas, plantains, sugarcanes, betel, pepper, and tobacco. These plants include both perennials as well as annuals, and so households are able to have a supply of food available throughout the year. An allotment may even provide a surplus that the household can sell or barter in the market in Viqueque town (Metzner 1977: 136–137).

The second kind of plot is the garden *(to'os).* Gardens are plots of land cultivated in the swidden fashion described above; their owners leave them fallow for several years while they reclaim plots that have lain fallow or make entirely new gardens for corn (the dominant crop), dry rice, tubers, and pulses. Corn takes from two to three months to grow and rice takes somewhat longer. To reduce the danger of starvation because of the failure of the rains to fall at the right time or in sufficient amounts, households interplant crops that have varying moisture requirements. Corn (which requires less moisture) is typically interplanted with cassava, pumpkins, and kidney beans. Dry rice is not usually interplanted as much as corn.

A household often cultivates two gardens, and these may be near the family home or several hours' walk away. Most Caraubalo villages have some residents who cultivate some plots of land to the east of the River Cuha or further south near the sea, in Maluro *suku*, Beaçu, and Rai Sut. But because it has a lower population density (resulting from its high incidence of malaria) than the other *suku*s near Caraubalo, the *suku* of Luca, several hours' walk west of the river, is much more favored as a location for Caraubalo gardens. One distinctive advantage residents of the village of Mamulak have in farming in Luca is that one of its component clans, Tuna, is credited with having its origins there and still is regarded as having rights to the land as well as kinship connections. Thus they have little difficulty obtaining permission from the local landowners to work the land in Luca.

Every garden usually has a hut, raised on wooden piles, which provides a shelter for members of a household during the times they are sowing, weeding, scaring away birds, harvesting, and threshing. The family also provisionally stores its crop of cereals in the hut until it is ready to be carried to the family home in the hamlet. Some gardens also have more substantial structures that give more comfort when the cultivators spend nights in the garden. Near their hamlet houses, families also build granaries in trees with protective shields around the trunks to prevent rats from scrambling up the tree trunk.

Both types of garden are enclosed by stout wooden fences to keep pigs and wild animals from destroying the crops, and making and maintaining these fences is laborious work. Since it typically takes two weeks to make a one-hundred-yard-long fence, it will take a single man about eight weeks to put up a fence around a 2.50-acre garden (Metzner 1977:126–127). The advantage of a kinship system in which male lineage mates are expected to cooperate in agricultural labor is readily understandable in the context of work, and quarrels that have their origins in the failure of kin to pull their weight are often bitter.

The Cuha Basin is well known in East Timor for its many coconut trees, and Caraubalo offers local subsistence farmers some opportunity for earning money from copra, the *suku*'s principal cash crop and a serious source of income since the early 1960s. For the first three or four years households tend to cultivate palm trees in gardens tilled by the *so'a rai* technique, and afterward they leave the trees to fend for themselves.

Coconuts were a feature of the Timorese landscape even before the Portuguese arrived, but only by the efforts of Governors Celestino da Silva (1894–1908) and Filomeno da Camara (1911–1917) was the palm tree established as a cash crop (Metzner 1977:217). When the administration reduced the level of its commitment to this attempt at transforming local economic life during the period 1920–1950 the interest of the local population waned. With the increase in the world price of copra toward the end of the 1950s the Portuguese renewed their attempts to convince the Timorese of the value to be gained from growing coconut palms, and in 1958 free seedlings were distributed to all who wished them. Because seven years is the average period coconut palms take to produce their first fruits, seven years later those seedlings had become fruit-producing trees, and the farmers appreciated the money the copra brought in. In Caraubalo six nuts are needed to produce 2.21 lbs. of copra, and it fetches a higher price than corn or unmilled rice, though not so much as milled rice (Metzner 1977:220).

Today, coconut trees, having replaced corn and dry rice, grow on the best alluvial soils of the River Cuha flood plain; elsewhere, too, where the soil is loose, flat land that used to be gardens is now under this crop. For about the first four years, the trees are interplanted with corn or dry rice, but as the palms grow, their shade inhibits the growth of the other crops. Since 1965 an increasing acreage of the more fertile soils formerly cultivated for food has been taken over by this cash crop, which is one reason why the amount of superior fertile land available for gardens in Caraubalo declined in the 1960s, a feature of the ecology that helps explain why Caraubalo families have gardens in other *suku*s.

Coconuts are harvested three times a year, with each tree providing an average of 20 nuts (Metzner 1977:223). The main crop is from November to February; the second crop is in May; and the third crop is in August. Boys or men pick the nuts from the palms or gather them after they have fallen to the ground of their own accord. The sale of copra has increased the amount of cash in circulation among the villagers, and some individuals are slowly acquiring more wealth than their kinsfolk. As individuals' wealth increases some kinsfolk are increasingly making demands for a share of wealth that was never part of the traditional system of rights and duties of kinship. These requests, which in some cases constitute outright demands, add their own weight to quarrels between males of the same descent group. Thus I would anticipate that the development of a cash economy will place increasing pressure on the already weak ties among members of the same lineages in Caraubalo, and will encourage the emergence of a social system in which bonds between males of the same patrilineal group will become even more tenuous than they were starting to become in the 1960s.

Animal Husbandry

The Timorese diet is supplemented by animal protein, which is provided mainly by chickens, whose meat augments a daily meal of vegetables. Pork is most commonly consumed on public occasions, and together with chicken constitutes the animal offerings made to spirits during household rituals. In addition to pigs and chickens, the Tetum raise horses and buffaloes, the latter of which are symbols of wealth in East Timor, as shown in a genre of *aiknananoik* whose plots typically include an episode in which a hero enters into contact with a nature spirit and returns from the encounter blessed by the spirit with an enormous abundance of buffaloes. In the 1960s Caraubalo had an exceptionally high number of buffaloes compared with most *suku*s in East Timor. Metzner (1977:186) estimated 21–30 buffaloes per 0.39 square mile as a conservative figure for the year 1969, which might appear remarkable considering the virtual absence of wet rice fields—and therefore employment for buffaloes—among the Tetum in the *suku*. The number of horses per square mile about matches that of buffaloes, but they render greater service because they are ridden and used as pack animals. What purpose, then, does owning a large number of buffaloes serve? The answer partly lies in the prestige that buffalo ownership confers on the owner and their use as exchange items given by wife-takers to wife-givers in marriage. In 1969 Caraubalo had roughly 527 buffaloes owned by 74 individuals, i.e., by 12.6 percent of the number of household heads (Metzner 1977:191).

The prestige of owning buffaloes in Caraubalo society may be part of the reason they appear quite prominently in the corpus of narratives I collected in this *suku*, and here is a story that puts Buffalo *(karau)* in an antagonistic relationship with Cat *(busa)* as mutual helpers in the work of gardening. Tetum stories are often verbal vehicles for conveying messages of a moral nature, and in the following episode we find the lesson of cooperation—or rather the failure of cooperation—spotlighted.

> Buffalo and Cat each had a garden, and one day they were working together at their task of weeding. They went into Cat's garden first and the two weeded quickly. Cat's mother cooked food for them to come and eat at midday. The next day they went to weed Big Buffalo's garden. At midday the two wanted to eat. Buffalo went off to eat grass. Little Cat asked Buffalo, "What am *I* going to eat? I am very hungry!" Big Buffalo replied, "If you are that hungry eat grass!" Responded Cat, "I don't eat grass. I eat rice. I eat meat. It would be better if you were killed, then I could eat your liver together with your heart!"

> Buffalo was very angry and went to the king to complain about Cat. The king ordered Little Cat to come to him. The king asked, "Little Cat, why did you curse Buffalo?" Little Cat said, "No, sir! I can tell you that I did not curse him. I am Cat and I can't eat grass. I am Cat and I buy rice and meat. I don't like to eat grass. I cursed him only by pointing out that were he to be killed I would like to eat his liver and his heart." The king said, "That's quite correct. Cat eats rice and meat. He cannot eat grass." The king ordered Buffalo, "Go and buy a buffalo, and kill it so Little Cat may eat!"

> Big Buffalo went looking to buy one, but he was unsuccessful. He returned to the king, who was irritated to hear him say, "I've just come back from my quest, I could not find one!" "You could not find a buffalo? Then you are as good as dead, for Little Cat may now eat your liver together with your heart!" Big Buffalo quickly imprisoned himself in his corral. He said to Cat, "Go, call your relatives, and bring them back with spears to kill me, so you can all eat me."

> Little Cat went off, hurrying to bring his relatives with spears, and they all came. They asked one another who was going to kill Buffalo. There was an elder among the cats, and it was he who took up a spear to strike Buffalo, but the cats saw that Buffalo had not made his corral with ordinary wood. He had remade it with dry wood that was

easy to smash up. So he had broken out of the corral that had "imprisoned" him, and had escaped. All the cats could do was to look for him in his house. But Buffalo wasn't at home. He had run off to sea. So the cats had no buffalo meat to eat, and so had to eat whatever they could find in their homes.

Timorese pigs are regarded in an altogether different light. They are ubiquitous in hamlet life and are allowed to wander around foraging at will, though since they are a threat to the crops grown in the gardens they often wear collars of bamboo tied around their necks to prevent them from passing through holes in garden fences. Despite this precaution, it is not uncommon for a pig to squeeze through some gap or other to feast on whatever crops it can get its teeth into, thereby bringing about one of the most frequent causes of trouble between neighbors.

Pigs have no prestige in Tetum society and in stories they are often associated with food. This theme dominates the next narrative, which is unusual in that it credits pigs—or at least a most singular pig—with what might be interpreted as a soul and introduces the notion of reincarnation, a consideration that rarely appears in Tetum imaginative thinking.

> A long time ago there was an old man and an old woman who had a son and a daughter. The son was called Lako Lekik and the daughter's name was Bui Lakok. Bui Lakok died, and after her death her soul returned as a female pig called Bui Lakok who gave birth to seven piglets. Bui Lakok said to the little pigs they should come to eat in her brother's garden. The piglets said they wished to. When they arrived in Lako Lekik's garden they found that Lako Lekik was himself hungry, and he caught the mother pig, his own sister. The seven piglets cried for their mother, who said to them, "Go, away! I am as good as dead!" The piglets said to their mother, "Oh, no! We shall be attacked by dogs!" Their mother replied, "It's better that you go, for I am as good as dead." This was true. With a blow, Lako Lekik killed the sow and carried the carcass home to roast—cutting every part of it up, and cooking it all. Lako Lekik said to all his people, "You may eat, but I don't want to." The people ate it all, and then he asked them, "Does it taste good or not?" They all said it tasted good. Lako Lekik said, "I didn't want to eat the sow because it is really my sister. I didn't want to eat." Everyone was sick because the meat was bad inside them, and they could not vomit it up.

One factor contributing to the buffaloes' prestige, I suspect, lies in the belief that credits them with a soul or *karau klamar*. Like the souls of agricultural spirits, the buffalo soul also resides in the underworld, yet can enter the material world to play a part in propagating life when ritually invoked. Upon entering the human world, buffalo souls take up residence in geodes corresponding to those adopted as residences by nature spirits, and they may form part of a stone complex known as the *fatuk maka*. The geode sits in a shallow saucer-like depression in an altar slab called the *fatuk knua* or "nest" sunk into the ground. This altar is normally located near its owner's buffalo corral and is said to give birth to baby stones— tiny slivers of stone fragments—whenever a buffalo cow belonging to its owner gives birth to a calf. Accordingly, a chicken is sacrificed to the buffalo soul in expiation of some purported offense if a man's buffaloes have not calved recently.[4]

The Division of Labor

Men, in general, have little to do with the domestic affairs of life, and the activities of a household are reckoned among the duties of the females living in the house. Among their daily chores women and girls collect water from the river early in the morning, bring it back home in pots, cook meals, dish them out, and afterward wash up. Weaving or plaiting mats and baskets at home fills up time for those individuals who have the ability or interest. A small number of women from clans that own the right to make ceramics sell these items, mainly pots and plates, and their agricultural produce on Sunday mornings in the market at Viqueque town. Their husbands, brothers, and adolescent sons sell or buy dried areca nuts, tobacco, buffalo meat, pork, spear blades, palm wine, or machetes. When selling is over the women usually head for the half dozen or so Chinese stores while men attend the cockfights. Women and girls also collect wild berries, nuts, and fruits from the woods and catch shrimps with small nets in the River Cuha. Most other tasks depend on the season of the year, so when the time for agricultural work arrives women accompany their men to the gardens and assist in planting, weeding, or harvesting.

Men, and boys old enough, catch fish with large nets, build houses, mend garden fences, clear the wilderness for gardens, plant crops, weed, harvest, slaughter pigs and buffaloes for food, and manufacture such artifacts as fishing nets, spear blades, straw hats, and silver ornaments for sale in the market. They also prepare areca nuts and tobacco.

Age and social class influence the Timorese division of labor. When the workforce for some communal task such as house building is more than adequate, the senior men take over the least physically demanding tasks, even at times relieving themselves from any work other than shouting advice or issuing instructions to their juniors. Ritual, too, modifies the assignment of responsibilities. Only married women in Vessa village may make ceramic dishes, for example, and only women of the Makdean clan in Uma Kik *suku* have the right to make pots. Weaving is the prerogative of a few aristocratic lineages and making lime (used in betel-chewing) may only be done by the postmenopausal women of Maneiku lineage in the village of Mane Hat. One might suppose that these rights would be justified in myths, but I was never informed that this was so.

Although there is no prohibition on their engaging in commercial activity in the market, prominent officeholders such as the *makair fukun* or *dato ua'in* and more educated men, like André Pereira, refrain from it, probably out of concern that their dignity might be compromised. Wives of prominent men, however, unless they are of royal rank or of the family of the *chefe de suku*, are not so inhibited.

The Seasonal Cycle

Figure 4 summarizes the normative seasonal cycle in Caraubalo. I wish to emphasize that the cycle represented here is only an ideal construct because one of the great problems of Timorese agriculture is that the rainfall on which farmers depend is precarious. In some years the rains are delayed by weeks or even months, and sometimes they fail to put in an appearance at all, with a consequence that can be devastating for villagers. In the year prior to my arrival in Viqueque the rains began in early November, then halted for several weeks with the result that the seeds planted in the soil during the first downpours failed to germinate.

The monsoons control the cycle of seasonal activity, and although little annual variation in temperature occurs, two wet seasons or *rai udan* and two dry seasons dominate people's lives. The wet season, roughly from November to June, is interrupted by the "little dry season" (*ua'i loro kik*) in February. The dry season proper (*ua'i loro*) starts in June and then continues until about the beginning of November. Figure 4 shows how closely the cycles of monsoon, work, and social activities should coordinate. But this is the ideal desired by the Viqueque populace who are only too aware that the rains are unpredictable.

The seasonal cycle in 1966–1967 also started promisingly in November like the preceding year and unlike the preceding year continued unabatedly. Toward the end of October the skies over Caraubalo clouded, and in a few days thunder and lightning heralded the advent of serious rains. By the end of November, the rains were pouring down virtually every day.

With the first drizzle of the wet season, members of most households leave their hamlets for their gardens and, supervised by the head of the household, the women, girls, and young men plant corn. The younger boys, as far as I could tell, usually neglect their responsibilities and play around or make excuses to stay in the dry garden hut with their fathers, leaving most of the planting to women and girls.

That year, when the corn had been planted, families planted cotton, cassava, papaya, sweet potatoes, yams, taro, peas, and beans. After their first garden was finished, the households moved to their next garden, scurrying or moving with more deliberation according to their sense of urgency, making their way, often with some difficulty, along the muddy paths. Most households had planted each of their gardens by the middle of December, and they returned home or remained on successive nights in their garden huts weeding. The floods sweeping down from the uplands during the rainy season when Timor is under assault from the Northwest Monsoon renders the River Cuha unfordable and frequently virtually submerges the bridge at Viqueque town. Bridle paths may be more than a yard deep in mud and practically impassable. Natural conditions such as these mean that only between the closest of hamlets is much traveling done at this period by the residents of Mamulak and Mane Hat, and then only between those who live on the same side of the river. In the dry season a villager who would take five minutes to walk from the hamlet of Fatuk Mean Craik to Cailulik, for example, might take over thirty minutes in the wet season.

In February 1967 the rains slackened off, and in the first few dry days families that had planted promptly when the first drizzle arrived were already able to harvest their corn. Families that had waited until they were convinced the rains had really arrived had to wait until March for the corn to be sufficiently ripe to harvest. Others were even doing so in April. The corn is harvested principally by women and girls, who pluck the ears of corn from the stalks, throw them into baskets and when they are filled carry them on their heads to the garden hut. Young men may help with the transportation of the corn and also help their mothers and sisters sort the corn into ears that are to be used to replant the crop when the time comes, corn that will be kept for later consumption, and corn that is to be consumed in the near future. The senior men may also help since this work can be conveniently done while they are sitting down in the hut.

When he first makes a garden, a household head builds a stone altar (fuluman) at its center and then dedicates it to the corn soul, who is regarded as "the guardian of corn and garden." Betel juice and chicken meat are then deposited on the altar to induce the soul to take up residence within. Thereafter, twice a year, the household will perform the ritual of "making the corn come alive" (halo batar moris) shortly before the annual rains are expected, in late October and then again in late March. The ritual's stated purposes are to make the union of rain and seed fertile and to protect the growing crops against rats (cf. Hicks 1984:78–82).

I was told that in the past the corn could not be consumed until a ritual called the saun batar, "to secularize the corn" or "liberate it from the taboo (lulik) against picking it," had been performed. When all the corn had been collected men went in search of a person whom they would sacrifice to the soul. The proposed victim could be of either sex, and a child was as acceptable as an adult. When a solitary person was found, he or she would be bewitched in some way and rendered helpless. The victim would then be seized and his or her tongue slit open. The blood from the wound was dripped into a bamboo tube and was taken to where the ears of corn were being kept and the blood was sprinkled on them. After this bloody aspersion a feast would be given at which chicken and pork would be consumed by those attending the ritual and some pieces given as a sacrifice to the soul of the corn. Three days later the victim would be killed. Blood, like betelchew, establishes communication between sacred and profane, stimulates fertility, and in ritual contexts conveys a sense of abundance.

When the harvesting is finished and the corn transported to the family house, men and older boys waste no time clearing away the detritus from gardens in preparation for planting rice, an activity that may take a couple of weeks, and is sometimes carried out as early as late March, though mid- to late-April is more usual. On 29 April 1967 the rice plants were between eleven and twelve inches tall in one garden near Nu Laran, whereas other gardens had only just been planted. Like corn, the planting of rice is mainly done by women and girls.

The rice soul *(hare klamar)*, characterized in chapter 2 as being another category of soul, is equally at home with both dry rice and wet rice, though, of course, almost all the rice grown by the Tetum in Caraubalo is dry rice. Like the corn ritual, the rice ritual has as its purpose to induce the soul to make the conjunction of seeds and soil fruitful, and the name by which it is known, *halo hare moris*—"to make rice come alive"—conveys this notion.

Between April and May households plant the second crop of corn, together with more root crops and beans, after which they weed until July and women and girls occupy their time throwing stones at birds to keep them from eating the growing crop. By now the rainfall is abating. Women and girls harvest the rice in August, and when they have completed their task men and boys thresh it before storing the crop away. Kinfolk help each other in the work, and when mutual help is not available they pay neighbors to assist. A family often finishes its threshing and storing of the harvest in a single day, and the feast that celebrates labor's end often offers the occasion for a cockfight. In August families collect areca nuts, bananas, tobacco (which is cut up and dried in the sun to be sold as a cash crop in the Viqueque market), kidney beans, cashew nuts, papaya, and cotton. Cassava is the most visible crop remaining when all the harvesting for this month has been done. Corn is harvested in August–September, and the gardens are fired to clear away the weeds that had accumulated over the season. The soil may then be tilled through October, and garden fences repaired. With onions and pumpkins still remaining unpicked in the soil, the annual cycle closes.

Let me stress again that this is a normative view of the cycle of the seasons. The monsoons are unpredictable, and even in an ideal year, the quantity of grain stockpiled in a family's house is usually sufficient only to just meet its needs until the next harvest. Thus, should their reserves be less than hoped-for, the risk of starvation for a household becomes very real indeed. Here, of course, lies the advantage of root crops, which have a greater tolerance of rainfall variability than cereals; but even these may not suffice to fill a family's needs, and sometimes households are reduced to the expediency of eating the corn they had put aside to plant for the next season's harvest. The family's deficiency in this way perpetuates itself into the following year.

Temporal Succession

From what I have said it will be clear that the main temporal division in Caraubalo—as in all of Timor—is between the dry season and the wet season, but these two divisions are themselves segmented into smaller units or months (*fulan*). These are lunar in reckoning so do not correspond exactly to the Western sequence of calendar months.

At the level of the day and night, although traditional culture lacked mechanical means of gauging the passage of time, observation of the movements of sun and moon provide the Tetum with the means of temporal division and these divisions are given conventional associations. Noon is an important transitional division, when contact between sacred and profane is especially likely to result in transformations of spirit into human and human into spirit as in the origin myth of the Tuna clan. Myth also plays a part in indigenous notions regarding the division of the day, and we see in the myth of the fight between a pair of birds, summarized on the following page, how daylight and night came to be of equal lengths.

Gregory Forth (1992) has drawn attention to a theme he has shown to occur in certain narratives among a number of ethnic groups in eastern Indonesia. In these tales two birds are pitted against each other as they fight to determine how long daylight and night should be. One of the contestants, friarbird, wants a short day alternating with a short night, that is, the existing mode. This wish is consistent with the character of the friarbird's voice, which consists of rapid, short calls. His antagonist, whose own call is slower and of longer duration, favors a long day alternating with a long night or, in some versions, a long night alternating with a short day. In all the tales, whatever their version, it is friarbird whose choice prevails—day and night of equal lengths. The special interest of my own Caraubalo version is that it is *friarbird* who favors a long day alternating with a long night while his antagonist desires a short day alternating with a short night and that—although it is not entirely clear how he can be considered to have lost the contest—friarbird does not get his wish.

Another obscurity lies in the precise identification of the two birds. There are several species of friarbird in eastern Indonesia, and some are found on Timor. The most plausible candidates for the species mentioned in the Caraubalo text are the Timorese friarbird (*Philemon inornatus*) (Coates and Gardner 1997) and the *Philemon timorensis*, which Costa (2002:182) identifies as the *kakoak* (alternative forms: *kako'ak*, *kaeko'ak*, *koakau*), which is its name in the myth I collected and which he describes as a small, grey bird lacking head feathers. Its name, which is said to represent its cry, would seem related to the term *kako'a*, "to be in a hurry," "to hasten" (Hull 1999:154). In the Caraubalo myth the other bird is attributed the name *kaoá*. In their respective dictionaries Cliff Morris (1984:101), Ramos da Silva (n.d.:52), and Raphael das Dores (1907:138) identify this bird as a crow, but although it has black feathers (the origin of which is accounted for in the narrative) this identification is probably incorrect. Two Timorese, Mr. and Mrs. Constâncio Pinto, with whom I raised the matter, were convinced the *kaoá*, despite its black feathers, is not a crow, while the Costa dictionary (p. 187) and that of Geoffrey Hull (p. 170), which designate what appears to be the same bird as a *kaoá-lelok* and *ko'a-lelok* respectively, describe it as being a "small swallow." Given this uncertainty I prefer to retain the indigenous term in my synopsis of the narrative.

> In the beginning there were two wild birds. One was called *Kaoá*; the other was called Friarbird. They ate some fruit at midday. Then they came home. They roasted bananas in order to eat. They ate. *Kaoá* poured wine. The two drank. They became drunk. They began talking. Friarbird said to *Kaoá* these words: "I prefer this world to have seven days of light followed by seven nights of darkness." Then *Kaoá* said: "Why can't we have one night followed by one day? A day lasting seven days and a night lasting seven nights we definitely can't have because we would suffer too much. Therefore I prefer one day followed by one night." Friarbird did not want this: "I prefer a day lasting seven followed by a night lasting seven." *Kaoá* continued to disagree: "It's like this. We shall become hungry. We must not suffer. Therefore it will be one night followed by one day." Friarbird hit *Kaoá*. *Kaoá* hit Friarbird with a gourd. Friarbird's entire head become covered in blood. Friarbird took some banana charcoal and rubbed *Kaoá* until he was black all over. Whereas Friarbird's entire head reverted to its normal coloring, that of *Kaoá's* remained black, for he couldn't wash himself clean.

The Sacred King

The fickleness of the monsoons makes it readily understandable that the Tetum would invest some imaginative resources in rituals designed to mitigate their lack of empirical control over the climate. Nevertheless, by the time of my fieldwork rituals of rainmaking were rarely practiced, but when they were carried out the figure responsible was the *liurai lulik* or "sacred king." His most important function is controlling rain, but since I have elsewhere described this aspect of his office (cf. Hicks 1984:84–86), here I shall describe certain of his other functions.

The office of sacred king descends patrilineally, with aptitude and personality modifying the principle of primogeniture. The position traditionally existed at both kingdom and *suku* levels, but with the dissolution of the kingdoms, the office at the kingdom level probably fell into extinction, though I did hear of the whereabouts of two sacred kings in Caraubalo. One, a 50-year-old-man from the lineage of Tula Kelu, in the village of Lamaclaran, has held office for fifteen years; the other lives in the hamlet of Leri, near Vessa village. Significantly, both are commoner villages, the social rank that at the *suku* level tends to be entrusted with ritual duties.

In the neighboring *suku* of Uma Kik there is said to live one sacred king, a man who lives in Makdean village in a locality known as Fatu Hada. The former kingdom of Luca, to the west, also has its sacred king, who is called Lu Leki, and who is credited with owning much gold. In ancient times, two other sacred kings, brothers (Naha Nunuk and Kai Nunuk), lived in Ossú de Baixo, a *suku* north of Caraubalo in the sub-district (and ancient kingdom) of Ossú. They are famous in myth for having established the boundary between Viqueque kingdom and Ossú kingdom near Mahuma.

In local Viqueque mythology, however, the name and deeds of one sacred king dominates the rest. Sacred king Hussi Rubik lived in the former kingdom of Bibilutu, at a place known as Ribu Lutu or Ra Tahun in a *knua* aptly called *knua lulik* (sacred hamlet), south of Caraubalo. This sacred king is credited with having died and become resurrected six more times during the course of one year before being eventually laid to permanent rest in *knua lulik*. These successive miracles were apparently brought about by local villagers digging seven holes in the ground around his grave and placing a pitcher of water within the imaginary circle they formed.

A sacred king is blessed with the power of attracting wild animals. All manner of creatures—birds, deer, and wild pigs—come to him when he calls. His charms also work on coconut trees for he apparently has no need to ascend them like ordinary mortals, but just asks them to drop their fruits down onto to the ground.

> As a further token of the power a sacred king is credited with having, there is a story about how the Portuguese government sent the sacred king of Luca to jail on the island of Atauro for some (undefined) political offense. When the ship arrived at Dili to collect him, it could not reach the shore on account of the high waves. But the sacred king

made the sea open up and then walked on the ground to the island. Later he was also able to extract himself from the trouble he was in with the authorities.

Each sacred king at the kingdom level was protected by two or three warriors or bodyguards, characters sometimes of a distinctly singular aspect. The bodyguards owned by one Viqueque sacred king were called Naha Iku La Tassi and Karau Ferik, the latter being a female buffalo. One of the Luca's bodyguards, Berei Mata Hat or "Berei of the four eyes," was said to possess a pair of eyes in the back of his head so that he could look to the front and to the back without turning his head. The three bodyguards who protected the sacred king of Bibilutu, Hussi Rubik, were all women. Their names were Hare Manek (Hicks 1984:8), Bui Taluk, and Oha Taluk.

A sacred king also acted as guardian of the ancient regalia sacred to the kingdom or *suku* on behalf of which he carried out his rituals. These were kept in the local ritual house.

Viqueque's Economy

With the exception of coconuts, people in Viqueque grow no cash crops, but they have some potential to work for an employer, though they are reluctant to do so and in any case there are few opportunities since only a small minority of persons can read or write. The jobs that are available include laboring in the gardens owned by the Chinese merchants, working in some capacity for the administration, or working on the roads. Since such jobs are by no means considered desirable, in order to repair bridges and roads damaged by the wet season rains *corvée* labor is necessary to keep the infrastructure operational. The administration obliges the *chefes de suku* to order every able-bodied man to work on the roads during the drier and less busy part of the year, from May to September, and it pays fixed wages. During this period Caraubalo men may move to other *sukus* to avoid being conscripted for what is generally regarded as a disagreeable imposition.

Attachment to the Land

The attachment and security that characterizes the attitude of Mamulak and Mane Hat people towards their land is ritually enacted when a man undertakes a journey. The nurture he has experienced in the *suku* and the safety it furnishes contrast strongly with the indifference attributed to the outside world. When a man or a boy who is old enough to travel from his clan for any substantial length of time—to visit distant relatives, to go to boarding school, or, in the past, to go to war—a small plate covered with a lid (the *hanek matan mutin)* and a small water jar (the *u'e lolo oan)* are placed high up among the beams of the *uma lulik* where they remain until he returns. Since few *uma luliks* remain in Caraubalo, the back room of the residential house suffices in the majority of cases.

The father or some other senior man in the traveler's lineage places a *hena mean tahan ida*, "red piece of cloth," in the *hanek matan mutin*, and on top of this cloth puts seven slices of areca, on which he places seven betel leaves. He next pours cold water into the *u'e lolo oan*. The elder then places a second set of seven slices of areca and seven betel leaves in the *hanek matan mutin*, as before. When the traveler departs one set is removed and placed in his pouch so that when he is away, should he feel ill, he will be able to take a single piece of areca and a single betel leaf and chew them to bring about a cure (cf. chapter 2). He must later replace them with another pair so that there will always be seven areca slices and seven betel leaves in the pouch. Meanwhile, back in the *uma lulik* the *hanek matan mutin* and the *u'e lolo oan* are kept undisturbed, except for the water being topped up with fresh water as it evaporates. The *hanek matan mutin* must be white—the color of life and health—for this ritual and with no markings of any kind blemishing its uniformity.

Before the traveler departs, a small pig is killed and its liver inspected. If the hue of the liver is red this is taken as an auspicious augury, and the traveler is free to leave without care. A black liver is taken as an inauspicious sign that the traveler will meet with trouble. A white liver is a sign that the ancestors are angry. A man or boy will not leave unless his journey can be guaranteed to be auspicious, and so the elders keep killing small pigs until eventually one displays a red liver. Since the quest for an auspicious liver can prove expensive after three or so pigs have been slaughtered, the elders resort to killing chickens. Families that are poor in pigs may even ignore pigs in the first place, and start their prognostications with the less expensive animal.

Whether pigs or chickens are killed, however, the meat is consumed only by the household since the ritual is considered a family matter rather than one involving the entire clan. Nor is the slaughter of the animals regarded as a sacrifice to the ancestors. A liver may be white and the spirits be "angry," but it would appear that the family sees no need to appease them. This being the case, the animals slaughtered do not have to be red in color, as is invariably the case when sacrifices are offered to spirits of all categories. As Rubi Loik put it, only when people want to "talk to *lulik"* do they have to offer red pigs, red buffaloes, red chickens, and red rice. A small piece cut from the liver, together with six small pieces cut from any part of the rest of the meat, is placed in the *hanek matan mutin* to make a total of seven pieces of meat. In size and shape these pieces are identical to the slices of areca.

Although there is no sacrifice as such, the elders then pray *(tota)* to the ancestors, opening with a couplet that begins many such orations:

Oh! Na'i bei (Oh! Lord grandfather)
Oh! Na'i nai (Oh! Lord grandmother)

And then affirming the life-giving force of mother and father, and acknowledging the sustaining presence of the land that brings the mother and father together in fruitful union, they chant:

Rai ina (mother earth)
Rai aman (father earth)

The elder who has assumed the role of ritual leader then places two betel leaves together and dips them into the *u'e lolo oan* and with the wet leaves touches in succession the traveler's right shoulder, left shoulder, and center of the forehead.

While the man is away, his sisters are prohibited from having sex. If a sister does so, various kinds of misfortune will befall the man. A soldier might be "beaten" by a superior officer, for example, or a student might fail his examinations. Her offense may be expiated by the sacrifice of a pig or chicken, a rite that is also performed in the normal course of events when the traveler returns from his journey. The *hanek matan mutin* and the *u'e lolo oan* are retrieved from the places they had been put and placed anywhere in his house. As Rubi Loik once remarked, they can no longer "do any harm." What I take this to mean is that the *hanek matan mutin* and the *u'e lolo oan* are surrogates for the traveler only during the time between the first feast that sets him on his way and the second feast that signals his return. Any damage to them or the evaporation of all the water serves to bring mishap to him.

Informants gave me the impression the key element of the ritual resides in the water contained in the *u'e lolo oan*. Cool water in Tetum ritual signifies health and fertility and to be cool is to be in good health. The jar stands for the body of the traveler, the water for his soul. If the water remains in the little vessel he will remain healthy. In contrast, to be hot is to be ill, and if the water evaporates the implication is that the body is hot and it is clear to all who look that the "soul," that is, the water, has left the body, a departure that indicates a state of mental dissociation, trance, or death.

In former times if a warrior had been slain, his pouch was brought back by one of his kinsmen and hung up in his house. In the event the pouch could not be found, his *tais* (a sarong-like piece of woven cloth worn by men and women) would be hung up and another pouch obtained. Whether he returned from the war or not, a buffalo would be slaughtered.

The feelings of concern that attend traveling to distant parts are well summed up in a short *aiknananuk* that expresses the attitude of kin and spouse who await the traveler's return:

> A man goes on a journey
> His bed is just a bamboo leaf
> His pillow is just a bamboo root
> His bed is only the bamboo leaf.

Traveling is, for the vast majority of Timorese, very much a male activity. Although daughters of *liurai* families may go away from home to a religious school for higher education. Women tend to be traditionally more associated with home:

> The mother gives birth to the son
> She gives birth to the daughter
> The son travels to other lands
> The daughter remains in the house.

Although males are more at liberty to travel freely and females are expected to remain close to the hearth, the ritual with the plate and water jar also reminds its participants of the obligations attending the relationship between brother and sister and of the connection between her fertility and his welfare. It affirms the bonds of kinship between the sexes and of the fact that they are *feto fuan, mane fuan*—"fruit of the woman, fruit of the man," my topic for the next chapter.

Endnotes

[1] The six Tetum-speaking villages and their respective 1966 populations are: Mamulak (360), Mane Hat (496), Vessa (251), Cabira Oan (310), Has Abut (235) and Lamaclaran (199). Sira Lari has a population of 160. See Appendix

[2] In 1969 Caraubalo had 101–150 persons per 0.39 square mile (Metzner 1977:11). "[O]ver the period 1959/1960–1969/1970 this has increased 2.1–3.0% more than in any *suku* south of Ossú" (Metzner 1977:252).

[3] Here we find the names "Rubi Rika" and "Lera Tiluk" apparently assimilated into one personage; or it might be that there were two *liurais*, which to my knowledge, however, would be unprecedented in local tradition.

[4] I discuss the major annual ritual dedicated to the buffalo soul in *A Maternal Religion* (1984:73–83).

Chapter 4

Fruit of the Woman, Fruit of the Man

In this chapter I describe the organization of relationships, including that between human beings and their ghosts, governed by the indigenous idea that certain kinds of rights, together with their concomitant duties, devolve to those next in a patrilineal line of succession.

The People of the House

Ema uma laran, or "the people of the house," is the term for those individuals who reside together under the same roof. The most tightly knit unit in Tetum social organization, the household typically includes the head of the household, his wife, her cowife or wives, their unmarried children, one of the husband's widowed parents, and perhaps some more distant or destitute kin. In some cases, the household head's married children and their spouses will also reside in the house. In contrast, some houses may be occupied by only a single adult, who may be perhaps a widowed individual. Most households have no more than about seven members, but large dimensions can be reached by some domestic groups, that of André Pereira's being a case in point, for he was responsible for no fewer than nineteen persons. André Pereira looked after his thirty-eight-year-old wife, Hílda; two sons, fourteen-year-old José and eight-year old António; two daughters, Rosa (five years) and Domingas (four years);

71

and thirteen others, including his widowed mother and his paternal grandfather's brother's son's daughter.

A household head, his wife, and preadolescent offspring sleep in the back room of the house. In the middle room sleep unmarried females, and in the front room sleep married females of the house, their husbands and children (if their marriage is of the *habani* kind [chapter 5]), and everyone else. Nonrelatives sleep on the verandas; females on the rear veranda and the adjacent part of the lateral veranda. Males sleep on the frontal veranda and the adjacent part of the lateral veranda.

André Pereira is an influential man in village affairs, as well as being something of a personality in Baria Laran lineage, and if being in charge of a huge household does not in itself raise a man's political standing, it does enhance a household head's prestige, provided, as André Pereira does, he discharges his responsibilities conscientiously. Within the household the father exercises considerable authority over his dependants, within reason organizing their lives according to what he judges to be in the best interests of the entire household. For most economic tasks, including harvesting, planting, buying and selling in the market, and for daily chores, the household is self-sufficient. House building, fencing gardens, threshing rice, and clearing undergrowth preparatory to making a garden are tasks that require additional help.

The intensity of the relationships between members of the same household engenders tensions that may lead to quarrels, but age and sex differences, reinforced by daily interdependence and the undisputed authority of the household head, tend to tamp down open strife. The husband *(la'in)* is responsible for representing his household to the outside community, as, for example, he does at the annual census conducted by the administration, and however ineffectual a leader at home, in public, at least, he is held accountable for the conduct of his wife *(fe'en)* and dependent children *(oan)*. The father is also expected to be his children's disciplinarian.

A son *(oan mane)* is expected to defer *(ta'uk)* to the father in private as well as in public. Failure to do so may amount to a serious a breach of discipline, and is liable to provoke spiritual as well as physical sanctions by way of punishment, such as sickness brought on by the household head's ghosts. This deference includes the son refraining from addressing his father by name, striking him, or interrupting the flow of the older man's conversation in public. Respect *(ta'uk)* is partly a function of the educative role of the father, for one of the duties of fatherhood is teaching a son the responsibilities he will assume when he becomes a full member of his clan. Such responsibilities involve helping the father and the father's patrikin in such chores as house building, repairing garden fences, looking after buffaloes, and representing his father (and clan) on public occasions.

A daughter *(oan feto)* respects her father no less than does her brother, although for a girl her mother replaces the father as the major educative force in her life. Both daughters and sons regard all the clansmen of the father's generation with much the same type of respect they show the father and they address and refer to the clansmen by using the same term of relationship—*tei* or *aman*—as they use with the father. The expected relationships between a mother *(nain* [alternative: *inan*]) and her children differ from that of the father. The daughter's relationship with her mother has a certain respectful edge that resembles the father–son relationship. Since the mother is her daughter's instructor in her duties, and on occasion her disciplinarian, while generally amicable, theirs is a more taut relationship than the more relaxed relationship between mother and son, whom the mother rarely disciplines, deferring instead to her husband. The relationship between grandfathers *(tei tuak)* and grandmothers *(nai fei)* and grandchildren *(na'in oan)* is warmly affectionate, lacking any disciplinary elements, and is the same between great-grandparents *(ubu la'in)* and great-grandchildren *(ubu oan)*, though persons of the senior generation in this latter relationship rarely live long enough to see their great-grandchildren.

The husband and wife are mutually respectful partners in life's trials, and whatever the intimate realities of their relationship, they jointly present a harmonious unity outside the household. The husband–wife relationship serves as a paradigm for all relationships that imply balanced integration of mutual rights and duties. People say, as I noted earlier, of the *dato ua'in* and *makair fukun* that they look after the people of their *suku* as husband and wife look after their household. A wife's duties differ significantly from those of her husband. She runs the household and takes responsibility for offering sacrifices to the household ghosts, who are, of course, not her own but the patrilineal ancestors of her husband. As an outsider who comes from another descent group, the wife is in a parallel position to the ghosts of the house, since the ancestors are also outsiders for they are no longer mortals yet are still linked by ties of kinship to the household head. In ritual matters she is head of the household.

Entirely different is the relationship between elder brother *(maun)* and younger brother *(alin)*, which is more akin to that between father and son. The elder brother occupies a higher position in society, and their relationship serves as an analogy for many relationships of superiority–inferiority and authority–subservience, both pervasive features in Tetum thinking. The younger brother must show respect towards his elder brother similar to the respect a son shows to his father. When the older lad reaches adolescence he may issue orders to his younger brothers with the expectation of obedience and is entitled to precedence over his juniors when it comes to taking a place or being served at feasts. The older son inherits the bulk of the father's wealth and has the right to be considered first choice to suc-

ceed the father as incumbent of any secular office the senior man may
have occupied. The duties binding brothers are compelling and they mirror those between males of the same generation in a clan, who are also
classed as *maun* or *alin* depending upon their relative ages. Perhaps it is
the implacable character of these duties that tends to make the elder
brother–younger brother relationship one of stereotyped hostility, for
social life is notable for occasional antagonisms between male siblings,
often arising from failure to help kin with bridewealth, work in the gardens, or house-building. The oral histories of Caraubalo contain dramatic
tales of hamlets breaking up as the result of friction between brothers, one
or more of whom secede to found new hamlets.

The relationship between elder brother and younger brother finds
another analogy with that existing between members of different sexes.
The elder brother has more authority in secular affairs, as in law, political
jurisdiction, and matters of inheritance, and as such is a commanding figure in the profane world of the Tetum, conveying a persona that is unam-
biguously masculine. The younger brother, on the other hand, has
associations with the sacred world of ghosts, spirits, and the mother goddess, and whatever ritual paraphernalia his father may own he generally
takes possession of when the older man dies. But since the sacred is also
associated with the female sex, there is a link here between femininity
and the younger brother, an association that may help explain why the
elder brother typically addresses and refers to his younger siblings, without regard for differences of sex, as *alin*. Implicated in this identification
is the convention that a younger brother *(alin)* may substitute for a sister
(alin) or a mother when a group of males has no female available to make
sacrifices on their behalf to spirits, as might occur when a group of brothers are traveling away from home.

Brothers and sisters have a relationship marked by superordination
on the part of the brothers, whether younger or older than their sisters.
In public, and even in the privacy of their home, sisters are expected to
exhibit deference toward brothers who, if older, are responsible for
them. Otherwise, their mutual attitudes tend to be characterized by a
sense of reserve.

___

Descent

Although birth automatically confers membership of her father's lineage on a girl, her brother acquires only what might be termed "potential
membership." Effective membership, that is, being entitled to rights within
this descent group, is granted only after the kinsmen of his father's lineage
have agreed to collect together the items that make up the bridewealth,

and thus enable him to marry in an exemplary manner. A bridegroom is not permitted to contribute to his own bridewealth, and most bachelors would not, in any case, have sufficient resources. A man hoping to marry is therefore at the mercy of his senior kinsmen, who contribute bridewealth only if they believe he is likely to prove a cooperative member of their descent group, a clansman who will do credit to his lineage and honor his lineage commitments.

When a bachelor's father informs senior members of his lineage that his son wishes to marry they consider how diligent he has been in recent years in rendering help to them. Diligence is considered a realistic index of how conscientiously he will function as a mature man and member of their group. The lineage may not be a strong corporate body of men and women, but its individual members would like to think they can—even if only as a matter of principle—draw upon the services of their fellow lineage mates when necessary, and of those individuals related to them by genealogy none are more vulnerable than young unmarried men who will someday require bridewealth in order to marry. Established agnates tend to make the most of this vulnerability, and apart from death rituals the preliminary discussions between an aspiring bachelor's father and his male kin regarding their willingness to contribute bridewealth are one of the few occasions in which one witnesses the lineage operating as a group.

I suspect, too, that in their estimation of his worth, they consider if he would make the grade with their ghostly kin since a careless acceptance of an unworthy new recruit might bring about retribution from the ghosts at some point in the future, and it is as well to avoid misfortune of this sort. Ancestors serve as sanctioning agents against an irresponsible willingness to accept an unpromising newcomer into the ranks of their kinship group. The same can be said of the wife-givers and the person of the bride herself, who also must pass muster with the ghosts of the prospective wife-takers.

Among the Tetum the patrilineal descent group theoretically owns property in common, principally the land bequeathed to it by their founders who settled down on it, and has access to distinctive political and ritual privileges, which may include offices. In order to keep the agnates together, thus preserving the descent group's political strength in the wider community, after marriage brides leave their fathers to reside with their husband. For this right (among others) the bridewealth is given. In addition to the right of the groom to remain with his father's kin, giving bridewealth also entitles him to his bride's domestic work. However, the most important right from the perspective of the household and descent group is the right to claim the offspring of the marriage.

Although the generational transference of rights tends to be patrilineal, this does not apply to all types of property or in all situations. Some property can pass through women, especially utensils of the household.

Nevertheless, Tetum procedures regarding inheritance are as pliable as most of the normative ideas that influence their actions, and a person has quite some scope for maneuvering his or her property to someone he or she considers worthy of beneficence. If a man has no sons, his brothers' sons normally inherit his wealth; should he have no brother, the sons of the male kin closest to him in his own generation will inherit from him.

The property in which rights are invested can be tangible (money, jewelry, pigs, gardens, houses, and so on) or intangible (eligibility for political or ritual office, membership of a social class, and potential membership in a lineage). Property can also be classed along another axis: whether it is secular or sacred. The house, clothing worn in daily life, tools, and eligibility for political office are examples of secular property, whereas ritual paraphernalia and eligibility for ritual office would constitute sacred property.

As I have noted Tetum rules regarding inheritance are quite flexible. A dying man will invite his sons together and discuss the inheritance with them. Once he has made up his mind about how he wishes to allocate his property he tells them what they can expect. He calls the elders of his lineage to him and informs them of his will. After his death they ensure that his wishes are honored. Generally speaking, the eldest son receives the bulk of the property, including the house and the most desirable garden—the most desirable in the sense that it is the most productive, or the largest, or the most conveniently situated. Daughters usually receive nothing, although if her husband resides in the deceased's hamlet, a married daughter might receive something that her husband assumes responsibility for. If there are other gardens they, together with the allotment located near the deceased father's house, are normally left to the other sons. The widow and unmarried sisters are looked after by the sons. Mothers pass along their property in a corresponding fashion to their daughters.

After marriage most young men apply themselves to the task of becoming self-reliant so that a son who has not inherited a garden will as soon as is convenient after marriage select a suitable plot of land on which to make one. His kinsmen are obliged to help him, more especially those closest to him. For this reason, should soil, topography, and space make it possible, he tries to site his garden near his hamlet, but this can rarely be accomplished since the more fertile, alluvial, soils, will already have been taken. Because of the distance involved, his kinsmen might have too far to walk, so the *serviço hamutuk* (to work together), as the reciprocal assistance between kin is termed, he actually obtains may turn out to be meager, and thus at the beginning of his married life, relations with his fellow kinsmen may already have soured. He will get his garden going, perhaps with help from in-laws or friends, but he may have to pay them for this help. As his household expands in membership and its need for food increases, he will make a second garden. The scarcity of suitable land means a father may allow his married son use of his own allotment, at least for the first few years of the latter's married life.

"Fruit of the Woman, Fruit of the Man"

The term *"feto fuan, mane fuan,"* designates what is most suitably referred to as a lineage since it is a segmentary component of a more inclusive descent group *(ahi matan)* or clan. *Feto fuan, mane fuan* can be literally translated as the "fruit of the woman, fruit of the man," an evocative reminder, to its members that their group is a product of human fecundity. Obligations between its patrikin are less pressing than among members of the households that compose it, but as we have seen these obligations are nonetheless serious enough, and they are enforceable. Outside of the household, a man's *feto fuan, mane fuan* contains most of those individuals he most readily turns to when he wants help in some endeavor. However, it is only in comparison with clans that lineages can be said to command strong loyalty from its members, and as I remark below, friendships between individuals often outweigh descent group membership.

The *ahi matan* is comprised of a number of other *feto fuan, mane fuan* in addition to a man's own *feto fuan, mane fuan*, who, of course, contain more genealogically distant patrikin. These are scattered about in hamlets that are more dispersed than is the case with lineages, some of whose members are assorted into only two or three hamlets, or even in some cases, one hamlet. Members of the same lineage are normally more likely to be in daily contact with each other than with kin in other lineages of the same clan, and it is usually the wife-giving and wife-taking *feto fuan, mane fuan* that carry out the bridewealth negotiations, rather than the *ahi matan*. That an individual, or at least a man, identifies himself most readily with his lineage rather than with his clan is suggested by the fact that one common source of gossip at funerals is over which *feto fuan, mane fuan* sent representatives and which did not. An unmarried woman identifies herself unequivocally as a member of her father's *feto fuan, mane fuan*, but after her marriage, which in virtually all instances would be with a man in one of the two villages, her status is ambiguous. While she never gives up her membership in her father's lineage she nevertheless becomes assimilated into that of her husband to the extent that she carries out sacrifices to his ancestors, works about the house with any unmarried sisters he may be taking care of, and in general cooperates with his female kin. Some notion of her ambiguity is shown by the fact that a married woman is expected to observe the food taboos of both her father's and her husband's descent groups.

Besides denoting the most inclusive form of descent group, the term *ahi matan* is employed in two other senses. In one sense it refers to the hearth, which consists of a set of three upright stones within which the fire is kindled and on top of which the cooking pot is placed. In its second sense it functions as the indigenous equivalent for what the Portuguese call *povoação*. This is most likely a derivative sense since the traditional settlement pattern in Timor before the Portuguese imposed their system of administration consisted of dispersed hamlets or *knua* (cf. chapter 1). When the administration bundled together groups of hamlets into *povoações* to make the collection of statistical data more convenient and to suit other bureaucratic requirements, the Timorese needed an indigenous verbal marker with which to identify the new units. So they extended the range of meaning of their term for clan and hearth.

As the denotation for a descent group the term *ahi matan* refers to a social unit defined in part by the possession of an origin myth, culture hero, food taboos, and distinctive ritual behaviors. Persons of the same *ahi matan* are called *ali-maun* (*ali* = younger sibling; *mau* [*n*] = elder brother) or *mau-alin*. The term includes an array of relationships, ranging from that between the youngest sibling and his or her elder brother to one between younger and elder members of the same generation in the same clan, who are all considered *ali-maun* or *mau-alin* with respect to each other.

One particular interest during my field research was investigating the functions of these descent groups, most especially as they related to the ownership of land and the contraction of marriages. Given the fact that these functions are verbally prominent in the lives of villagers, their impact on social life is surprisingly slight. Individuals know the various myths of origin that register the deeds of their ancestors and willingly trace the genealogical links between the more celebrated of their ancestors as well as those of their more immediate living kin, but when it comes to social action, the lives of individuals are governed by personal bonds they have forged (for personal reasons) rather than by jural compulsions or the weight of tradition. Because persons who spoke about their traditions more often than not referred to their distinguished ancestors' mythological doings and clearly identified themselves as part of the same group, I assumed at first that the lineages—if not the clans—must therefore operate as corporate social groups in such enterprises as contracting marriage alliances and forming political affiliations, as well as each one representing itself as a unit at collective ritual gatherings like birth and marriage. This did not prove to be the case, however.

Establishing these alliances and attendance at most communal rituals in the practice of social life was for the most part the responsibility of individuals rather than the descent group, usually those most personally involved in the events. True, the presence of a representative of the descent group was in principle required, but the entire group itself was rarely involved. Funeral rituals are somewhat different. They are the most important and well-attended of all collective gatherings in Caraubalo, but even so at the funerals I attended not all lineages in Mane Hat and Mamulak sent representatives. Even then the descent groups merged their identity into two groupings, the "people who [give] life" and the "people of death," that were only in part defined by descent (cf. chapter 7). Individuals would stress the importance of marriage alliances between lineages, and informants insist that men of the same lineage were responsible for assembling the bridewealth when a young man from their group wanted to marry, but in practice only those who wished to do so or who could not evade their responsibility contributed (cf. chapter 5).

Consistent with the absence of a strong corporate ethos among individuals belonging to the same descent group is the slight interest I found in genealogies. Although, as mentioned above, villagers can find genealogical links between prominent personages in the line of their ancestors and know where they figure into the genealogical network of their contemporaries, more expansive links do not appear to engage the interest of individuals or have much social importance. A comprehensive genealogical recollection for three generations can be reliably forthcoming from many persons, but further back only the famous are recalled. Furthermore, although some females (e.g., Cassa Sonek, and certain famous queens) do figure in genealogies, given the patrilineal tenor of the society, the recollected names are generally those of men. This obliviousness to generations further back includes famous families, for although great names may not be entirely eclipsed by time, their precise place in family histories is frequently contested.

While individuals vary somewhat in the degree to which they wish their memories to stretch back over time, in a collective sense the seventh generation is a conventional cut-off point for clan genealogies. Like the numbers two, three, and four, the number seven has symbolic significance in Tetum culture and appears in many rituals and narratives, in contexts involving the notion of unity. In genealogical histories the seventh generation is as far back as clans are said to go, so that names previously representing generations are routinely discarded or coalesced with others to retain the hepatic pattern. Consistent with the founder of a clan always being spoken of as having lived several generations ago, both José Pereira and his father, André Pereira, would say that the founder of their clan, Tuna, the Eel clan, who was Lelasou, was seven generations removed from them. The same formula operates when the past incumbents of a political office, such as that of the *makair fukun*, are recalled. People typically speak of the first officeholder as no more than seven generations distant.

Coresidence is for the most part a more important influence on a person's daily life than genealogy, and while residence is in large measure a function of descent it can also result from personal decisions made by a multitude of individuals and have little bearing on paternal heritage. Therefore, when in this book I refer to a clan or lineage cooperating in what appears to be a collective enterprise, unless I specify to the contrary, I am referring to individuals representing their own interests or those of individuals in their descent group rather than the descent group acting as a corporate body.

At its level of maximum inclusiveness, the village of Mamulak, as we see in figure 6, is dual in structure, consisting of the Tuna clan and the Ina-Aman clan. Ina-Aman, whose name, "Mother-Father," implies both its authority and its prestige, has the higher rank. The clan—its bifurcated name speaks to the dualistic character of Tetum classification—consists of five lineages whose names in descending order of prestige are Ina-Aman, Kia Mahan, Balidi Mahan, Fatuk Mean Craik, and Nu Laran. The name "Ina-Aman," therefore, applies at both the inclusive level of the clan and also at the more exclusive level of the lineage. The clan traces its founding to the three Caraubalo heroes, Rubi Rika, Lera Tiluk, and Cassa Sonek, and it owns the territory occupied by Mamulak village. The junior clan, Tuna, is, of course, the immigrant descent group whose ancestor Lela-sou, according to one myth, obtained land in Beloi Soru from the leader of Ina-Aman, and in another myth (noted previously) obtained land from Rubi Rika and Lera Tiluk. As I remarked in the previous chapter, strictly speaking, contemporary members of Tuna are tenants of Ina-Aman clan and thus inferior to it, though in daily life—as distinct from myth and certain modes of ritual behavior—one might never notice this inequality. In descending order of prestige, Tuna clan's three lineages rank Bua Laran, Baria Laran, and Cailulik.

The organization of Mane Hat village, which consists of the superior Mane Tolu clan and the inferior clan of Makdean (figure 7), reaffirms the dualistic cast of Tetum classification. Mane Tolu is superior to Makdean because the first people to settle in what is now Mane Hat were members of Mane Tolu clan, with Makdean people coming as later immigrants. Makdean clan does not have sufficient members to split itself into lin-

Figure 6. The Mamulak Descent Groups

eages, but Mane Tolu, with its greater numbers includes three, which in descending order of prestige rank: Manecawaik, Maneclaran and Maneiku. Their names translate as "elder brother," "middle brother," and "younger brother" respectively.

The map in figure 5 shows that with the exception of Bua Laran lineage and Baria Laran lineage, the *feto fuan, mane fuan* in the two villages spread themselves over at least two hamlets. Ina-Aman comprises two hamlets; Kia Mahan, four; Balidi Mahan, five; Fatuk Mean Craik, six; Nu Laran, ten; and Cailulik, three. In Mane Hat village members of Makdean clan live in two hamlets. In the clan of Mane Tolu, members of Manecawaik lineage reside in one hamlet, Maneclaran in one hamlet, and Maneiku in four hamlets (the hamlets of Dau Bua Mahan, Caibowki, Betuhun, and a hamlet for which people apparently had no specific name). In both villages this pattern of dispersed residence results to some extent from overpopulation (cf. chapter 3) and fissioning brought about by quarrels between male kin. The demographic character of Mamulak is shown in figure 8.

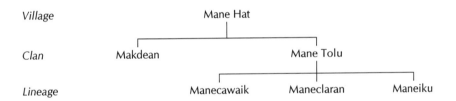

Figure 7.   The Mane Hat Descent Groups

Lineage	Hamlets	Households	Population
I. Ina-Aman Clan	2	5	22
Kia Mahan	4	13	60
Balidi Mahan	5	11	43
Fatuk Mean Craik	6	11	41
Nu Laran	10	21	96
Clan total	27	61	262
II. Tuna Clan			
Bua Laran	1	8	40
Baria Laran	1	4	33
Cailulik	3	9	40
Clan total	5	21	113
Hamlet total	32	82	375

Figure 8.   Mamulak Demography

Myths justify the claims each clan makes for its economic, political, and ritual rights, and within Caraubalo an individual's social status largely derives from the status of his or her clan and lineage. Clan membership determines to which social rank one belongs—whether one is an aristocrat or a commoner. Likewise, a man's prospects of playing a prominent role in the *suku* or in the village are a function of the hereditary rights his clan traditionally is credited with having, though his own talents and ambitions in some cases can mitigate against these limitations. Positions of the sort I am discussing, incidentally, are exclusive to men. Thus, Ina-Aman clan owns the office of Mamulak village headman *(dato ua'in)*, and within the clan it is the highest-ranking lineage, Ina-Aman, that in theory more directly controls this office. In practice, political expediencies trump theory, and should Ina-Aman lineage prove unable to provide a competent incumbent, a candidate possessing more ability even from another lineage would be considered. The office of deputy headman is conventionally credited to Kia Mahan lineage, but again pragmatism may in individual cases determine otherwise. In Tuna clan, Bua Laran lineage controls the office of secular leader, and Cailulik lineage owns the office of sacred leader, an office absent from Ina-Aman lineage.

I have drawn attention to the dual trend in Tetum classification, one, by the way, that is characteristic of all Timorese ethnic groups, but Timorese thought also follows a triadic format in some contexts and both modes of classification may be juxtaposed or even convergent. In cases where the three units in question are segments of clans, a characteristic way for them to be denoted is as eldest brother, middle brother, and youngest brother (as already noted in respect to Mane Tolu clan). When people talk about the internal segmentation of the Eel clan they also may refer to Bua Laran, Baria Laran, and Cailulik as "the oldest brother," "middle brother," and "youngest brother," respectively, thereby conveying the relative rankings of the three descent segments.

Cooperation and Conflict

As I have remarked earlier, rights and duties are most compelling within the household, and although kinship protocol is a strong sanction against ignoring requests for help, in many activities outside this social unit personal relationships exert more influence than customary law. Genealogical distance, too, is a factor. A man from one of the three Cailulik hamlets, for example, would not expect a kinsman in Bua Laran or Baria Laran to help him as readily as he would a kinsman from Cailulik lineage, and he would demand assistance more expectantly from a resident of his own hamlet than from one in the other Cailulik hamlets. The nature of the task is another element that is considered when making a request. No one outside your own lineage is obliged to help you build a house or garden, or raise bridewealth for your son. However, if you are arraigned before the village court by a person from another clan, every kinsman in your own clan would be expected, if only verbally, to support your position. Here, again, personal circumstances matter. If you are respected as a kinsperson who promptly and willingly assists others, you are more likely to find reciprocation when you need assistance.

It is in circumstances where customary obligations are at their most implacable that most social discord occurs, such as between kinsmen who live near one another and who work together. Disputes that are the most disruptive and frequent follow the contours of kinship distance. Conflicts between older unmarried brothers, in particular, who still share their father's residence are perhaps the most common, though the father–son relationship is also fraught with the potential for hostility. Excuses for not complying with the rules of reciprocity between kinsmen are legion, and evasion is a frequent fact of social life, thus engendering quarrels of lingering bitterness. Nevertheless, clanspersons realize reciprocity is a reality of social life and it is said that ghosts punish those who ignore traditional rules of mutual help or maintain festering relations with kin. Nevertheless, conflicts are usually resolved one way or another, usually by a respected senior man mediating between the contending parties. But should the issue persist to an unacceptable extent, relationships between the parties may deteriorate so badly that one or even both (if their quarrel has rendered them *persona non grata* to their coresidents) eventually may have to establish new residences elsewhere. Of all the occasions for cooperation and conflict, the most highly charged emotionally is that which occurs when men are asked for contributions towards the bridewealth of a kinsman's son, a topic to which I shall return in the next chapter.

Authority within the Descent Groups

Genealogical standing in large measure influences the allocation of authority within the descent groups in that within each lineage there is usually a group of kinsmen who, by virtue of descent from a certain ancestor, have the right to exercise authority as chief officeholder in the group. Individual circumstances may prevent his assuming authority, but generally speaking an eldest son's pre-eminent position in the family is again in evidence since members of the lineage tend to regard him as the natural successor of a deceased incumbent. However, this is far from being a hard-and-fast rule. Disinclination to assume the burdens of office, incompetence, or possessing a dubious character are among the impediments disabling an ideal succession from occurring, and it is not unusual for the lineage to ignore the eldest son and select as incumbent a man from another family in the lineage, however remote his genealogical links may be from the family that traditionally provides its leadership. Since everyone born in the lineage is by definition related by no more than a few generations, in the majority of cases the links would not be at all remote. The choice of incumbent, when it is made, comes about from a consensus reached by the adult members of the lineage, married women as well as married men offering their opinions, though men are usually more prominent in publicly airing them.

Public authority lies in the hands of married men, elders who in Viqueque are referred to as *bahen* as often as they are called by the term commonly used in other parts of East Timor, which is *katuas*. Unmarried men with years of maturity behind them may come to exercise some degree of influence in affairs and acquire substantial influence, but their impact on decisions has to depend on their force of personality, not their status. Accordingly, elders are rarely younger than twenty-three years of age, below which age few males will have married. Being of elder status is a prerequisite for holding office, and most chiefs are well over thirty, although the deputy chief of Mamulak village was only twenty-five in 1966.

Just as lineages look for their officeholders in certain families, so the clans of which they are constituent units find their officeholders in certain lineages, which means that the leadership of a clan tends to come from the dominant family in the dominant lineage. Again, the same contingent factors that come into play in specific circumstances emerge when it is time to choose the chief of a clan. Because in this case a larger number of persons is usually involved, selection is frequently a more formal process. There may be a meeting of all interested married men in the house of one of its clansmen—women do not normally partake in these formal discussions—if more than one candidate is in the running, and if a consensus does not emerge, an election day will be designated. Women as well as men then vote, each voter dropping a grain of corn into a basket where the votes are recorded representing her or his choice of candidate, with the winner emerging as the new incumbent.

In a village consisting of but a solitary clan—the case with five of the seven villages in the *suku*—the clan chief is *ipso facto* village headman, but Mamulak and Mane Hat, of course, each have two clans. Ina-Aman clan provides the village of Mamulak with its headman, as well as the *suku* with its *dato ua'in*, while Mane Tolu clan provides the village of Mane Hat with its headman, as well as the *suku* with its *makair fukun*.

According to one mythological version, the political system was determined in *rai moris* or "when the world was living or born," the name given to the timeless period when the fundamental order of the world was established and the prime necessities of human life became—by revelation or discovery—accessible to humanity.

> The narrative contends that the lineage that is Manecawaik or "elder brother" was given the office of *makair fukun* when he (a person known as Manecawaik) visited the kingdom of Luca, a few hours by foot to the west and the most prestigious kingdom in the region. The elder brother (Manecawaik) passed the office down patrilineally until there were no longer any more men left (or qualified) in his line to serve as incumbents, and so the *bahen*, "elders," elected Funo Loik who came from another family. From Funo Loik the mantle was passed to Lequi Rubik and then Fono Kaik.
>
> The *liurai* of Caraubalo was around at that time as well as the *dato ua'in*. The *makair fukun* is the *liurai's* "father" and the *dato ua'in* is his "mother." The commoner descent groups of the other Caraubalo villages were part of the political system. The *makair fukun* is male; the *dato ua'in* is female. The *makair fukun* wields the scepter of the *fukun* and the *dato ua'in* wields the cord of the *fukun*, both scepter and cord symbolizing authority. When disputes take place, the *dato ua'in* and the *makair fukun* act as one. The masculine judgment and the feminine judgment make their decision together. They listen to everything; they judge everything in the courts like a mother and father. Their authority to decide questions is good. They may not be angry with each other; they may not be mad with each other.

This charter myth states that the office of *makair fukun* was originally granted to a man of the Manecawaik lineage, which lost the office because of its inability to find an incumbent after three men of this lineage had occupied it. The myth gives no indication of what lineage assumed control over the office or even if that lineage, too, lost it in subsequent generations, but figure 9 lists the last seven incumbents, beginning with Lera Funak. In 1967 there was a change in incumbency, with Fono Loik being replaced by Loi Lequik, both members of Maneiku lineage in the clan of Mane Tolu. The list shows that not only has Manecawaik not provided any incumbent in the memories of villagers, but that even the immigrant and junior clan Makdean has provided two.

The prime qualities for being a successful candidate for the offices of *dato ua'in* and *makair fukun* include knowledge of tradition, integrity, and possessing a "wise head." Having a wife who knows how to play the role of a good hostess is a decided advantage. The choosing of a *makair fukun* or *dato ua'in* lies within the provenance of the men and women of their respective clans, but clanspersons take into account the fact that they are choosing not just the chief of their clan but also a political figure who will occupy one of the two most responsible political positions in the *suku*.

Incumbent	Clan	Lineage	Hamlet
Lera Funak	Makdean	Makdean	Makdean
Kai Mutin	Mane Tolu	Maneiku	Caibowki
Fahi Lequik	Makdean	Makdean	Makdean
Fono Kaik	Mane Tolu	Maneiku	Dau Bua Mahan
Lequi Rubik	Mane Tolu	Maneiku	Betuhun
Fono Loik	Mane Tolu	Maneiku	Dau Bua Mahan
Loi Lequik	Mane Tolu	Maneiku	Betuhun

Figure 9.   Succession to the Office of *Makair Fukun*

They thus willingly listen to the views of chiefs and elders of the other *suku* clans, more especially their counterparts in Mamulak or Mane Hat, as the case might be. If the succession is contested, the elders of the clan discuss among themselves, in informal sessions, the rivals' strengths and weaknesses; only if elders have not been able to reach a consensus in this way do they meet in council where each man makes his views known. Should the council meeting fail to result in a consensus acceptable to a decisive number of elders, an election is held along the lines described above. Women vote and express their opinions outside of the council, but formal discussions in the council are carried out by married men.

Within the *suku* the *makair fukun* and *dato ua'in* are the highest arbiters of any disputes that may rise to that level and that come under traditional jurisdiction, but as I mentioned in chapter 1, transcending the indigenous system of justice is the legal system by which the Portuguese authorities administer the colony. Disaffection with a judgment made under the indigenous code occasionally makes one who is party to a contention seek the chance to better his lot with the *liurai*. If the *liurai* is satisfied with the original decision or considers the matter too trivial to concern him, he may decline to review the case, and the decision reached at the lower level stands. Disputes, like all important matters of concern to the community, such as discussion of succession to the *makair fukun* and *data ua'in*, are formally arbitrated in the council house *(uma bo'o)*, which is located in the hamlet of the *dato ua'in*. The *suku* council of elders then becomes a court, and the elders assume the responsibility of advising the *makair fukun* and *dato ua'in,* who now function as judges.

Wars between kingdoms and between *sukus* were common Timorese dramas before 1912, and the local kingdoms of Viqueque, Bibilutu, Luka, and Loi Huno were each involved in alliances that harnessed the aggressive impulses of their respective *liurais*. Below the level of the kingdom, the *suku* chiefs played a major role in assembling the fighting forces upon which the kingdom *liurais* depended. In Caraubalo this responsibility fell to the lot of the *makair fukun* and *dato ua'in*. The ritual dimension of warfare was, as we have seen, handled by the priest (cf. chapter 2).

Although a chief is the executive authority within his own political segment, what might be considered the ultimate authority in the traditional political jurisdiction resides within the body of elders *(bahen)* within the group in question; also it is these elders who have responsibility for finding a fresh incumbent to fill the gap left by the death or retirement of a chief and for removing an incumbent who has forfeited the confidence of his constituency. During my fieldwork the *dato ua'in* was well-regarded by the community of Mamulak, but his father, who preceded him in office, had been removed in 1955 at the age of fifty-five by the village elders who claimed he had developed autocratic tendencies. The displaced chief thereafter became a recluse from politics and took no part in public affairs.

Removal of a chief is one way villagers can limit the power of these leaders; another is by emigrating. Like removing a chief, emigrating from a region because of difficulties experienced with the chief is not a common resort, but at times circumstances contrive to bring it about. The migration of Sira Lari people from western Balarauain in the period between the two world wars was brought about by dissatisfaction with how local authority was exercised, and the village of Has Abut was founded in Caraubalo by members of two Cabira Oan lineages who could no longer tolerate the disagreeable attitude of their village chief. In the latter case, the move diminished the prestige of the chief of Cabira Oan as it added a new village chief to Caraubalo *suku*.

Although the Portuguese administration had all but eliminated the traditional powers of the *liurais*, at the levels of *makair fukun* and *dato ua'in* traditional governance has remained robust since the role these figures play in the political system was not obtrusive to European authority, which mostly ignored—or remained in ignorance of—their influence in village life. Accordingly, although a crime such as murder or sedition fell outside the jurisdiction of the chiefs, a multitude of offenses still remained subject to their authority.

While constrained by the collective power of the elders, a chief's authority is also strengthened by it, whether the community is a lineage, clan, village, or *suku*. The elders do not form a coherent body of advisers that systematically considers issues and advises the chief; rather, it is a collection of individuals who sporadically find themselves available to offer advice on a particular issue. In rare instances a dispute may move up from one level to another, say from lineage to clan or from clan to village, but since villagers, on the whole, tend to respect authority, more often than not the decision of a chief at any level of governance, when it is clearly endorsed by the elders, will be accepted. However, should a dispute remain unresolved, the ultimate *suku* authority, the *liurai*, will settle the matter.

Death was the traditional punishment for murder and sorcery, while theft could be punished by cutting off the guilty party's hand. Nowadays, infractions of the indigenous code of behavior are punished by paying fines usually in the form of pigs. Common offenses involve owning pigs or buffaloes that damage a neighbor's gardens or fences or eat his crops, or physically assaulting another person. The guilty party may also be required to throw a feast for the plaintiff, which includes the slaughter of pigs or—if the offense is sufficiently grave—a buffalo. Depending on the nature of the offense and the standing of the guilty party, the latter's kinsmen may or may not help defray the expenses of the fine. If the party decides to take the matter to the *liurai*, his or her chances of getting support from kinsfolk diminishes; this tactic is thought to remove a controversy from a traditional authority to an external one, where alien traditions apply.

Thus far I have been discussing the living kin of a descent group, but in Caraubalo, people behave in their ritual lives as though their descent groups contain another category of kin, the ghosts or *mate bein*.

Ghosts

Mate bein are the ghosts of the ancestors, and of all the inhabitants of the spirit world it is these elementals that involve themselves most in human affairs. Every ghost, of course, must once have been a dead soul or *klamar mate* (see chapter 2), but people are not explicit about how the transition from *klamar mate* to ghost occurs. It would appear clear from the suggestions I was offered by my informants, however, that this transformation is brought about by the *keta mate*, a ritual carried out twelve months after the burial that permanently installs the soul in the sacred world. After the ritual is finished, the soul is referred to as *mate bein*, and never again as *klamar mate*.

The term *bei* [*n*] signifies something "big," "venerable," or "worthy of respect" and, as noted earlier, also refers to a person in the generation of the grandparents or higher. Other than the three founders of Caraubalo (Rubi Rika, Lera Tiluk, and Cassa Sonek), the only ghosts of much concern to an individual are those of his or her own descent group, and to only these ghosts are sacrifices made. The ancestors most generally sacrificed to are males: the father, grandfather, and great-grandfather. Regard-less of their sexual identity when alive, as mentioned previously, ghosts tend to be associated more with femininity than with masculinity, possi-bly because their spiritual abode, the sacred world, is identified so inti-mately with the earth mother.

Since ghosts are to some extent regarded as kin possessed of a spiritual nature, in much the same way as kinsfolk have a mutual responsibilities to help one another, so, too, are they and their human relatives bound by mutual obligations. Mortal kin sacrifice chicken meat, wine, and betel-chew to the ghosts, sometimes offering the sacrifices at places near cemeter-ies, which are a favorite haunt of these spirits, but most often on household altars within the confines of the hamlet. Dangling near the altar from a cen-tral beam that supports the house hangs a pouch called the "pouch of the ghosts," which provides a place of repose for ghosts, as well as a receptacle for these offerings when the ghosts visit a household. Sacrifices are part of the ongoing striving of human beings to coax the ghosts to make the sexual union of the husband and wife fecund, so that the man's *feto fuan, mane fuan* may be endowed with "the fruit of the woman, the fruit of the man." These sacrifices also persuade the ghosts to intercede with the guardian souls of plants and buffaloes to encourage them to make the union of seed and soil, as well as that of the bull and cow, productive (cf. chapter 2). Neglect in making sacrifices, however, invites ghostly retribution and meddling, which usually means sterility and sickness.

When they are glimpsed, these entities are usually construed in female form, though they are hardly a flattering representation of woman-hood. Their repulsive appearance and ungainly comportment contrasts with nature spirits whose feminine manifestations tend to be beautiful and elegant. Ghosts are said to be occasionally glimpsed at night, and those who have encountered ghosts describe them as plodding along on stubby legs, wearing a loin cloth, and having black hair covering their faces. They have unusually long arms and sometimes walk on tiptoes and stand more than six feet in height, an unusual height for a Timorese. But their brown skin color resembles that of the Timorese. Other villagers describe ghosts as resembling tailless monkeys that talk among themselves. They also converse with shamans when the latter wish to consult with them.

Like nature spirits, ghosts are regarded with caution. Although gen-erally beneficent, they are not part of the mortal world, and while they replenish the fertility of their descent group, they are swift to punish mis-behavior, which includes offenses of both omission and commission. Failing to place offerings regularly in the pouch of the ancestors, lapses in duties of kinship, and conducting oneself in such a way as to endanger the reputation of one's descent group are among the most common lapses that are likely to incur sanctions.

Ghosts are physically stronger than human beings, but they apparently harness their power only at night, at which time they take the opportunity to beleaguer miscreants when they are sleeping by stretching out their arms, seizing their throats, and squeezing them until consciousness is lost. Upon awakening victims are usually anxious to make a larger offering than usual of betel-chew or food at the household altar by way of expiation. If that expedient fails to allay further attacks victims will usually consult a shaman. Although they have the power to withhold fecundity from their human kin, ghosts, unlike nature spirits, souls of the dead, or witches, rarely inflict death.

Persistent misbehavior by members of a community sometimes triggers collective retribution. Contention between members of a hamlet is a common explanation for the fissioning of these settlements, and occasionally ancestors get involved, in which case it is not unknown for the entire hamlet to be forced to relocate. Such discordant episodes in *suku* histories may assume legendary proportions, with kin attempting to save face by blaming the ghosts for the relocation.

> The people of Bua Laran, claimed they had resettled themselves in 1960 in their present location because in their earlier dwelling place they had been persecuted by a rash of nocturnal disturbances brought about by ghosts. They gave in evidence the fact that the ghosts refused to leave the vicinity of their original hamlet after the *keta mate* ritual had been performed for an ever-increasing number of corpses. The people speculated that their ancestors were dissatisfied with the sacrifices that had been offered to them after the last few funerals had taken place. The kin and affines of the recently deceased rely to some extent on their ancestors deflecting a vindictive soul from visiting sickness on their community, and should the ghosts decide not to intervene, although the living can still put up ritual defenses against the marauding soul, they are decidedly more vulnerable to its depredations. The Bua Laran ghosts, I was informed, chose to withdraw their support from their kin, and so dead souls were free to batter away at the ritual defenses of the hamlet without restraint.

> Soon people were complaining about having nightmares in which they imagined dead souls entering their houses, and a rash of these apparently prompted a wave of hysteria that threw the population into a state of incoherent confusion. Then the ghosts joined in, until it seemed that not a night could pass without the sound of souls sobbing and ghosts whispering balefully. No ritual devices succeeded in mollifying the presumed anger of the ancestors or repelling the hatred of the dead souls. Months dragged unhappily on until one evening as they were returning from their gardens, some Bua Laran residents, emotionally taxed, spied a female form possessing incredibly long and immensely powerful arms swaying from side to side as it plodded threateningly toward

them on stubby legs. Black hair hid her face, and a loincloth hung from her waist. Details of this unnerving encounter became embellished with the retelling, to such effect that before many nights had passed sleepers began waking up at night shouting out that they were being asphyxiated by ghostly hands. These hallucinations proved to be the final straw, and in a despairing attempt to atone for their offenses the residents of Bua Laran relocated their hamlet a short distance away, where they were troubled no longer.

Although we cannot know with any degree of certainty what were the sociological or psychological factors that led to these fanciful episodes, a factor of some possible relevance is that Bua Laran lineage was said to be among the most Christianized in Mamulak. Since the early 1950s Caraubalo *suku*, like others in Viqueque, had been subject to proselytizing by the missionaries, one upshot being that certain educated villagers lost their faith in the authority of their ancestors, an apostasy that led to them refusing to offer any more sacrifices to their ancestors. Whether or not the people of Bua Laran were more radicalized than those of other descent groups, they were, people said, in the forefront of these changes. Thus, when the Bua Laran folk started complaining about nocturnal agitations, their more conventional neighbors understandably might have interpreted their afflictions as ghostly reprisals. Whatever the causes, the alarm generated by complaints reached a point when even the Christianized residents of the hamlet were overtaken by the hysteria, so that when the ghosts made clear their intention of remaining in the hamlet, their kin made the decision to establish a new settlement elsewhere. This sacrifice may have been sufficiently great to satisfy the ghosts.

The Ritual House

The *uma lulik* or "sacred house" is a building set aside for the storage of a descent group's sacred possessions, and it is that place more than any other where the interests of ghosts and kin most tangibly converge. There, material artifacts symbolizing the bonds that unite these two categories of kin are stored and public rituals of reciprocity by which ghosts and the descent group collectively satisfy each other's needs are carried out.

Before missionary proselytizing began to undermine the ritual basis of Tetum life and the Portuguese system of administration abolished the political foundations of the kingdom, each *suku* and each kingdom possessed a ritual house that represented their authority. Here, at gatherings presided over by either the *liurai lulik* or a priest, members of these respective communities would sacrifice to their common ancestors and contemplate their collective ritual heirlooms.

From the outside a ritual house presents an appearance hardly differ-ent from that of a typical Caraubalo house (Hicks 1984:33–38), though it is smaller, but inside there is a single room instead of the three compart-ments found in a family house. Stored in the room are the aforementioned heirlooms accumulated over the course of successive generations of ances-tors, and these typically include ancient swords, ornaments shaped like a buffalo's horn that are worn on a man's head, breast plates that hang from a man's neck, jars, plates, and pieces of Portuguese flags—all objects his-torically affiliated with the ancestors.

Ritual houses are said to have come down from ancient times, and I was told that they were built by the ancestors and that contemporary kin are not empowered to build new ones. They were an emblem of the group's claim on the land they occupied, ownership derived from a mythical con-tract with the nature spirits that lived in the region. Though immigrant groups might acquire permission from the landowners to settle down, they lack the entitlement to build a house of their own, so immigrant descent groups like that of the Tuna clan do not possess their own ritual house.

The ritual house is the most prominent representation of a descent group, and in Caraubalo only the two landlord descent groups in the *suku*, Mane Tolu and Ina-Aman, possessed these material representations of their collective ritual life. Mane Tolu's ritual house, the remains of which are located on land occupied by members of Manecawaik lineage, is credited with being the "strongest," but when I examined it in 1967 it was in a sad state of disrepair, having been smashed up years earlier to appease the missionaries. Some of the group's sacred artifacts were still preserved inside, however, including a machete, the broken remains of a sacred water jar, a coconut shell cup fastened to the end of a long wooden stick, a small fragment of old red cloth, and a dark brown, 3-inch-long grindstone, worn very smooth and used for sharpening the machete. This grindstone was said to have once belonged to the founder of the descent group, an ancestor by the name of Leki Fonok.

The building was orientated east–west, with the front door (the men's entrance) facing west and the back door (the women's entrance) facing east. Near a pillar in the women's section of the building stood a water jar inside which was a small, sacred, pebble. The remains of the Ina-Aman clan's building no longer exist.

The relative lack of social and ritual functions of the descent groups in Caraubalo, to which I called attention earlier, was brought home to me during my fieldwork by the absence of these buildings as operational units. As missionary success gathered steam and the offices of rainmaker and priest were abandoned, so were the ritual houses that their custodians had safeguarded during the centuries since the *rai moris*.

Chapter 5

Fertility and Its Gender

The system of traditional values of Caraubalo would appear to cast the respective procreative characters of males and females in different ways, and in this chapter I use the ritual of marriage and two other instances of ritual behavior, cockfighting and kickfighting, to demonstrate this difference.

In *A Maternal Religion* I draw attention to the fact that in the marriage ritual the ancestors are invoked and encouraged with betel-chew and other gifts to confer fertility on the bride and groom. I also describe how the ritual words uttered during the course of the stages by which the marriage comes about are replete with images of fecundity. The prayers recited during the successive stages through which the ritual progresses contain many metaphorical phrases that express the theme of fertility, among them reference to the bride as the "fruit" and "flower" of her mother's womb. The image of life-generating conjunction evoked in the term for "lineage"—*feto fuan, mane fuan*—is strengthened by persistent reaffirmation during the ritual, which imparts a multidimensionality to the image because the words chanted and the ritual gestures performed impress upon those participating in it that conjunctions of various kinds are also being made fertile. People of the descent groups of the wife-givers and the wife-takers exchange reciprocal pledges, and ghosts and kin reaffirm mutual needs as representative forces of the complementary, albeit opposed, concepts of *lulik* and *saun*.

The sexual act that underlies the creative potential of the ritual epitomizes this set of conjunctions, and the bounty of a fecund union is anticipated in the form of children, health, and abundance in general. This

93

image is sustained verbally when the future wife's father *(banin)* utters a little speech in which he refers to the bean tree and fruit tree as he urges the bridegroom to "carve an alliance" between the two descent groups, for these two trees represent the two groups. When their barks are sliced with a knife, both exude a reddish secretion villagers liken to the blood that carries the life of each lineage from one generation into the next, and the bloodstream of both groups, people say, converges in the baby that is to be the product of the marriage. In many rituals that deliver the theme of conjunction, blood itself may actually be spilt, as when a chicken, pig, or buffalo is slaughtered, but betel-chew—*buran* or, significantly, the "blood of the areca"—is more conveniently used, both ritual substances standing for life, fertility, and abundance in general.

In the dialect of Tetum spoken in Caraubalo the nearest verbal correspondent to the English-language verb "to fertilize" is *hahoris* (or *hahouris*), "to create," "to generate," "to breed," "to beget." This verb also means "to give birth to," and would appear related to *hamoris*, "to enliven," "to quicken" (Hull 1999: 102, 119), which conveys the sense of generating life in something. At the same time, the notion of fertility is also conveyed in a rather more diffused way by several other terms including *buras*, which conveys the sense of "thick," "abundant."

The verb "to reproduce," "to multiply," "to propagate," in the Tetum language may be translated by *belar*, a reflexive verb, as well as by *hadiki* (to sprout) or *nasaren* (to flower). A woman who is pregnant is said to be *feto ko'us*, with *ko'us* (used as both verb and adjective, but only for human beings) signifying both "pregnant" and "to conceive." An alternative term is *krahat*, and a woman who is pregnant is said to be *feto lolon krahat* or "woman with a full belly." Yet another term for pregnant is *issin rua*, literally, "two bodies." Pregnancy in animals, however, is *kabuk*. On the other hand, infertility in a woman is *klalók*, or *fuan faek* (to be without fruit) and again a different term, *kiuk*, denotes infertility in nonhuman animals.

Marriage

The aristocratic and commoner social classes are endogamous: members of the two *dato* villages, Mane Hat and Mamulak, may not—at least in theory—intermarry with members of the other five villages in the *suku*, which are, of course, inhabited by commoners. Yet, as we shall see when the composition of the death ritual for Kai Lakok is discussed, the convention of endogamy is not set in stone. Although, again in theory, members of the same *ahi matan* should not marry, in practice this prohibition is sometimes ignored, as it occasionally is within the *feto fuan, mane fuan* itself, which leaves the hamlet as the only social unit that might be considered reliably exogamous. However, villagers tend to draw the line at second degree cousin marriage within the *feto fuan, mane fuan*. Since mothers usually come from outside a child's *ahi matan* and a father's sisters will have married men from another *ahi matan*, first degree cousin marriage with a cross-cousin is acceptable. Indeed, for both young men and young women marriage with a first degree cross-cousin is a socially desirable one. In other words, a man would be marrying his mother's brother's daughter *(sai oan)* and a woman her father's sister's son *(maun or alin)*. For Mane Hat and Mamulak residents, as noted earlier, the majority of marriages take place among themselves.

Although the Tetum language has distinct terms for three quite different forms of conjugal unions, *hafoli, habani,* and *fetosá-umane*, given the social implications of marriage it is perhaps surprising that this institution is not marked by any generic term. In the context of marriage, the effective social unit in the majority of non-*fetosá-umane* marriages is the household with *ad hoc* groupings of kinsmen helping the respective parents of the couple. Senior men from a lineage are responsible for arranging marriages, including raising bridewealth, but although there is some sense that they are representing their group as a unit, these men put together the gifts on behalf of the father of the bridegroom rather than on behalf of their lineage, unless the marriage is one of *fetosá-umane* in which case the lineage does act as more of a corporate group. By no means will all senior men in a lineage contribute to the bridewealth. Whether a man does or not depends upon how close his kinship ties are with the father, how much the two men have helped each other in the past, his attitude towards the young man and his bride's family, and other such factors of circumstance.

Most marriages in Mamulak and Mane Hat are of a form known as *hafoli,* a regime in which the bridewealth secures for the young man's family all rights in the children and the right to remain living near his father after marriage. Since marriages have been contracted for decades in Mamulak-Mane Hat, probably a high proportion of families in each of the lineages in the two villages have affinal interconnections, so it would be somewhat misleading to say that any particular marriage plays a demonstrative part in maintaining affinal ties between the respective lineages involved. However, the sense that marriage involves more than the two households immediately involved is certainly more palpable when one talks to the villagers than in another form of marriage found in Caraubalo, namely, the *habani*.

The term *hafoli* means "to make up the bridewealth" *(folin)*. It is also known by the figurative term *na'an tolu*, "the three pieces of meat," so-called because the bridewealth has as its most important gifts the buffalo, horse, and pig. It also comprises an additional gift called the *pataca lima nulu*, "the fifty *patacas*," a *pataca* being an old Mexican coin the Portuguese introduced into Timor.[1] Although no longer circulating, *patacas* are among the most common ritual artifacts of a descent group. There is also a second set of gifts, the *modok*, "the green vegetables," a figurative term that signifies five *patacas* and a sacred cloth known as the *hena mean tahan ida*. The contrast made between the "meat" and the "green vegetables" corresponds to the Tetum distinction between cooked food (introduced to humanity in the origin myth of fire) and raw food, as well as to local culinary values that assign different qualities to meat and vegetables. Meat is regarded as "food" *(han);* vegetables are merely a supplement to food. No *hafoli* can take place without the "meat," but if the groom's group and bride's group are of roughly the same social prestige and the marriage is regarded as desirable by both, the "green vegetables" can be disregarded. Nevertheless, the Tetum consider it desirable that each of the aforementioned gifts be given. These gifts are the minimum for marriage. When marriages involve wealth or socially prestigious families, such as those of *liurais*, the actual number of beasts given can amount to dozens.

A bride married in *hafoli* brings her personal possessions and whatever domestic utensils her mother may have given to her when she moves to her husband's home. She will also inherit property from her mother when the senior woman dies. The *hafoli* does not bring the lineages of the man and woman into a formal relationship, as does a fully functioning *fetosá-umane*. It does, however, serve as a catalyst for like-minded individuals in the two groups, who wish to exploit the quasi-institutional possibilities for cooperative benefit by extending their social reach. Should a young man succeed in obtaining the support of his father's senior kin, his father collects the items that make up the bridewealth from them and delivers these items to the girl's father, who redistributes them among the senior male kin of his lineage. If a prospective groom fails to obtain bridewealth, he has one of two options: he can postpone marriage, in the hope that an improvement in his behavior may raise his standing with seniors (and therefore their willingness to contribute to the bridewealth) or he may go ahead and marry anyway, according to the protocols of the *habani*. Henceforth, he cannot demand help as a conventional entitlement from his kinsmen in the chores of daily life, and upon the death of his father he will find himself facing stiff competition from his brothers for his father's estate.

Raising bridewealth is the most negotiable duty of kinsmen. Even in a small lineage it is unusual for every senior man to contribute, but members who are outside of this group rarely make contributions. The closest kinsmen, for example, the father, the father's brothers, and married elder brothers, can rarely avoid the obligation of providing bridewealth, and failing in this duty causes serious friction between kin.

One celebrated quarrel in recent Mamulak history occurred between André Pereira and Rubi Loik. According to Rubi Loik's version of the events, André Pereira failed to contribute toward the bridewealth of Rubi Loik's eldest son in sufficient quantity to prevent the son enduring the inconvenience of having to reside with his bride's father in *suku* Uma Kik. His rancor was made all the more corrosive by the knowledge that when one of André Pereira's dependents, Leki Loik, had married, Rubi Loik was one of only a few men contributing to the bridewealth. Not long after his son's departure for his new home, Rubi Loik began publicly vilifying André Pereira, each recital of his grievance deepening his annoyance. At this time Rubi Loik happened to be domiciled in Bua Laran, just one minute's walk from Baria Laran, so that the paths of these two men often quite literally crossed and during their encounter they more than once confronted each other. Mutual vilifications eventually provoked a rousing brawl during which—according to André Pereira—only the intervention of André Pereira's mother stopped Rubi Loik from being killed.

My impression was that the majority of villagers tended to side with André Pereira, and this communal bias probably persuaded Rubi Loik to move to *suku* Uma Kik where he lived for a number of years until a quarrel with his affines induced him to return to Mamulak where he decided to live in a hamlet in which his was the only house. His house is the only residence in the hamlet, because, Rubi Loik claimed, disputes over stray chickens too easily occur if kin reside together. His relatives in Tuna clan, however, said his reputation as a trouble-maker discouraged others from accepting him as a coresident.

The entire "three pieces of meat," and whatever additional items may be added on to make up the bridewealth, can be given in full by the time the couple is established in the groom's house or, alternatively, with the consent of the woman's father, be given piecemeal over the next six or more months without the groom having to reside with his wife's father during the interim. To obtain this concession his family must hand over the "three pieces of meat" during the bridewealth discussions and make clear they have every intention of giving the remainder within a reasonable time. If a husband with children dies before his bridewealth obligations have been completely discharged, the children will be considered as belonging to their father's descent group, no matter if their mother takes them back to her natal hamlet or leaves them in her husband's, provided a close kin of the deceased man completes the bridewealth transactions within a period agreed to by both families.

The responsibility of paying off the bridewealth is said to fall primarily on the eldest brother of the dead man, but the scope for evading this duty is ample. Since the brothers themselves are not fettered by alliance ties to their deceased brother's affines, unless there is little bridewealth remaining the debt may descend to the next generation, and the next, a debt that may result in continual bickering between the descendants of the original partners. Until the total bridewealth has been given, the children, in principle, belong (either from birth or, if boys, potentially) to their mother's lineage. In practice, however, by the time there are only a few items outstanding, the children are regarded as effectively under the permanent control of their father's descent group, which, when a girl marries, keeps the bridewealth she brings in.

Protracted bridewealth payments normally indicate either the young man's group is too impoverished to keep its side of the bargain or that it has entertained second thoughts about the desirability of the marriage. Kinsmen may hope they can delay payment long enough that their prospective affines will allow them to evade the settlement; but if the woman's family is forceful enough the husband and his wife will eventually be obliged to transfer to his wife's natal hamlet.

As traditional styles of postmarital residence break down and individual circumstances increasingly determine where a newly married couple should live, the transformation is one of diminishing agnation and increasing cognation, with potential kinsmen residing with their fathers-in-law, a decline in the wealth of lineages, and a general sense of descent group dissolution as men earn money and become less dependent on their descent group. Descent in Caraubalo is evolving from the more restrictive mode of patrilineal dominance to one of nonlineal dominance, that is, cognatic descent. A traditional institution that might appear to facilitate this change from a society organized by patrilineal descent to one less restraining for the individual is the *habani*, the second mode of marital alliance.

While common enough, the *habani* is regarded by the villagers as a less desirable alternative to the *hafoli*. No gifts are given, for one thing, and it does not offer the same affinal potentiality or the same opportunities for making alliances. The young husband, in addition, goes to live with his wife's father in circumstances that, of course, vary from case to case but are rarely congenial since the junior man will never be a member of the senior man's lineage. Indeed, he is not regarded as a full member of his father's lineage either, and his children become members of his wife's family. By marrying in *habani*, a groom "makes for himself a father-in-law"; that is, apart from his wife, he creates his wife's father as the most influential person in his life, the senior man's influence being partly the consequence of the young man living in his house. Once he becomes a father, the young man is permitted to have his own house but must still reside in or near the wife's father's hamlet. The husband is obliged to share his wife's domestic services with her father, her unmarried brothers, and her mother. Lacking any standing in his wife's lineage, a husband who lives with his wife's parents finds himself in a subordinate status relative to his wife's father's kinsmen, the more senior of whom have authority to command his help in such activities as house building and gardening. For his part he can merely request help and hope they have the good nature to oblige. A daughter's husband is not entitled to any office in her lineage nor is he eligible for an office in his father's lineage.

The *fetosá-umane*, the third form of "marriage," is rarely practiced by the Tetum-speaking population of Viqueque, but it nevertheless is present in their thinking about how descent groups can be allied with one another, and the institution exists as an alternative to the *hafoli* and the *habani*. The *fetosá-umane*, also known throughout East Timor as the *bar-laque* or *berlaki*, is an institution very common throughout the island—in the west as well as in the east—and is a conspicuously influential one among almost all of the ethnolinguistic groups. The Viqueque Tetum are, with the exception of the Wehali Tetum, unique in Timor. in not having it as an effective institution, a lack that makes an ethnographic study of their social organization especially appealing since it gives us the opportunity to see how a Timorese society functions absent the most distinctive of all Timorese institutions.

This is not to say that the institution is not active anywhere in Viqueque. Communities that speak Makassai are famous for it, though the Makassai have their own term by which they denote the institution, and in Caraubalo it is represented by the Makassai of Sira Lari village. Nor is the *fetosá-umane* entirely absent from Tetum calculations, for a few Tetum families in the region are said to have *fetosá-umane* alliances in their recent histories, and Caibowki and Betuhun hamlets of Makdean clan in Mane Hat have a tradition of practicing this form of alliance. Furthermore in the ritual speech uttered at funerary celebrations *fetosá-umane* alliances are sometimes quite explicitly evoked. Some Tetum lineages also have *fetosá-umane* alliances with Makassai-speaking families. One example, noted earlier, is the Tuna lineage of Baria Laran, which is allied with a descent group from the ancient kingdom of Loi Huno, lying between Mamulak and Ossú, by virtue of André Pereira's marrying a Makassai woman who came from there.

Why the Viqueque Tetum do not exploit this institution is hard to say. The Tetum of Wehali, just across the border in West Timor and from whom the ancestors of the Viqueque Tetum may be historically derived, also lack, as I remarked, the *fetosá-umane*. Wehali, however, is a case apart since in Viqueque this system of affinal relationship exists at the very least as an institutional possibility whereas in Wehali the *fetosá-umane* is absent even from the ideology of the culture. One possibility, of course, assuming the fact that the Viqueque Tetum came from Wehali, is that they arrived in Viqueque lacking the *fetosá-umane*. In such a case, the presence, such as it is, of this institution among them might have resulted from Makassai influence. But there is no evidence to back this argument.

The Tetum themselves have no consensus on the matter, but some informants speculated that in the past the *fetosá-umane* had existed, before missionary activity eradicated it. Now while it is true that the River Cuha valley is more accessible than the mountains where the majority of the Makassai reside, missionaries elsewhere in East Timor proselytize in upland areas and even make converts without impairing the functioning of the institution.[2] Furthermore, the Makassai communities that reside on the more accessible southern plains have retained this custom.

The *fetosá-umane* differs from the *hafoli* in its asymmetric character. The two descent groups (whether clans or, more usually, lineages) involved in the marriage must be unequivocally defined as either wife-giver or wife-taker. In other words, a wife-giving group cannot take a woman from its wife-taking partner, and vice-versa, so that the relationship between the groups cannot be symmetrical—women from one group cannot be exchanged for women of another. This prohibition applies regardless of generation, which means that from generation to generation descent groups are related as either wife-givers or wife-takers. By contrast, in the *hafoli* the two groups are allowed to exchange women, symmetrically, so that a wife-giving group may also be a wife-taking group, as occurs, for example, when a pair of men marry each other's sisters. The *fetosá-umane* prohibits exchanges of this nature.

Although the *fetosá-umane* is ineffective as a social fact among the Tetum-speaking population of Viqueque, as I noted above, some descent groups claim to have such alliances in their traditions, and this relationship is referred to during death rituals involving the two groups (cf. chapter 6). Furthermore, some rules implicit in the *fetosá-umane* have some bearing on the way the *hafoli* is carried out. One of these is the choice of spouse. Although in the *hafoli* direct exchange between two lineages is permitted, sister-exchange between individuals in those lineages is strictly speaking regarded as improper. No secular sanctions exist, but the ghosts take note, and should the marriage, for one or other reason, be deemed a failure, local gossips have their explanation already at hand.

The obligations between the descent groups contracting a *hafoli* marriage are, as I have said earlier, fairly minimal; but affinal responsibilities are very real indeed in the *fetosá-umane*. Partners in an alliance of this nature demand considerably more than in the other two forms of marriage, and they are under stronger pressure to fulfill expectations to provide mutual help when called upon to do so—lending money or other material resources, perhaps, or backing in political maneuvers, or support in legal disputes. Ritual requirements involving gift giving and the saying of prayers for the other partner are part of what it means to be engaged in this form of alliance, and the descent group contracting it tends to act much more effectively as a corporate body than do the descent groups in a *hafoli*.

Another difference between the *hafoli* and the asymmetric *fetosá-umane* involves their symbolic characteristics, which are much more elaborated in the case of the latter. In the *fetosá-umane* the wife-takers are associated with femininity and the wife-givers with masculinity, as the etymology of the term *fetosá-umane* suggests. *Feto*, of course, denotes female, woman, sister; *umane* = *uma* + *mane*, "the house of the man" or "the masculine descent group." The meaning of *sá* is more obscure, but one possibility is that it refers to a kind of skirt worn by women. This masculine/feminine dichotomy is reinforced by the terms used to denote the alliance groups themselves. *Umane* remains as the term for wife-givers, but the term *fetosá* is replaced by *feto-oan* or "daughter." Hierarchy, as in asymmetric alliance systems elsewhere in the eastern archipelago, also appears here, since masculine is considered superior to feminine as the adult (father) is superior to the child.

Whereas in the *fetosá-umane* the status of wife-giver is superior to that of wife-taker, *hafoli* entirely lacks this sense of status difference; the possibility of the symmetry of the exchange logically means that both are prospective wife-givers and wife-takers to each other so that neither can be superior or inferior in an absolute sense. Another distinctive attribute of the *fetosá-umane* involves the symbolism of the gifts exchanged. The wife-givers give what are referred to as "feminine" gifts to their partners; the wife-takers reciprocate with "masculine" gifts. Feminine gifts include the bride herself, cloth, and pigs. Masculine gifts include buffaloes, swords, necklaces, breast-plates, curved head-pieces, and money. The idea that as the "masculine" partners the wife-giving descent groups receive masculine gifts and that as the "feminine" partners the wife-takers receive feminine gifts applies also at traditional birth and death rituals. Wife-givers and wife-takers attend the rituals that take place for their partners on these occasions, and each group gives to its alliance partner gifts of the same symbolic character as they give at marriage. Thus the descent group celebrating a birth or mourning a death receives masculine gifts from its wife-takers and feminine gifts from its wife-givers. Systematic gift giving of this nature is absent in the *hafoli*.

Breaches in the normative conduct of relations between the sexes are taken care of according to a variety of prescriptions. When her father notices that his unmarried daughter's stomach is beginning to bulge, he takes all steps necessary—including physically chastising her—to discover the identity of the culprit. As soon as he knows the offender's name, he sends out a pair of male emissaries known as the *maklaak manu ua'in* to the hamlet where the miscreant resides. The use of *maklaak manu ua'in* as intermediaries is customary in formal invitations between groups, such as when guests are invited to attend weddings and funerals, as well as in situations in which the potential for violence exists. Should the man refuse to marry the woman, he must compensate for the offense by giving the father a piece of store-bought cloth *(hena)* and a buffalo. If he decides to marry her the penalty is waived.

Other irregularities involving gender give us some insight into the relative statuses of men and women in Caraubalo society. In the case of rape, for example, if the victim is a married woman the offense is interpreted primarily as a blemish on her spouse's reputation. The rapist must pay a piece of store-bought cloth to the woman, but a piece of more splendid woven cloth *(tais)* in addition to a buffalo (a large pig may substitute) to the husband. The *tais* is given "to remove the shame" of the husband. As Rubi Loik remarked to me, the *tais* "cleans his face of the dirt and dust" that has stuck to him. That rape is construed as being directed more against the man than the woman is confirmed by the fact that should an unmarried woman be raped, the rapist must pay to her father the same penalty as if she had become pregnant as a result of a mutually agreed-to act of sex, that is, one piece of *hena* and one buffalo.

Allusions to fertility and the life that results from it are readily understandable in the context of marriage and sexuality, but allusions to these notions in situations where behavior might seem considerably more playful, such as in cockfighting and kickfighting, might seem something of a puzzle. Yet, as we shall see, these two sportive activities also provide a forum for expressing these notions.

The Kickfight and Cockfight

Manipulating the substance of blood symbolically in two violent sports (spilt from the body in the one; retained within the body in the other) offers a metaphorical means by which the Tetum refine their concept of masculinity. At the same time it empowers men with a quality that is inherent to the female sex as a fact of biology. Thus far we have seen that Tetum notions of human existence involve ideas concerning the sacred, fertility, life, and procreation, but this complex of ideas is augmented by other ideas that at first glance might appear directly antithetical. These comprise notions involving violence, headhunting, death, sterility, and blood, of which blood, I think, needs to be regarded as the key notion. When manipulated in rituals performed in Tetum society, blood is credited with the capacity to open what might be called "lines of communication" between sacred and secular, and this is the most prominent way in which fertility and life are infused from the former into the latter.

In stipulating the qualities that define masculinity, people to whom I spoke stressed courage and force, most flamboyantly celebrated in narratives describing headhunting expeditions. This was a practice that the

Portuguese authorities brought to an end after they established effective control over East Timor in the years that followed the final revolt of the local kings in 1912. The notion of manhood is also conveyed by the terms for "north" and "south." North is *tassi feto* (woman's sea) and south is *tassi mane* (man's sea), the ascriptions derived from the relatively tranquil nature of the Wetar Strait to the north and the more turbulent character of the Timor Sea to the south.[3] Exaggerating these traits of manhood, as in certain Mediterranean societies, however, is alien to the more restrained Tetum values.

Although Tetum men follow conventions that set them apart as a social category from women, at the same time a man may, at least to some extent, identify himself with the female sex without the risk of incurring social condemnation such as would occur, for instance, if he were to dress after the fashion of a woman. Despite such an easy tolerance, each gender is nevertheless associated with specific qualities, in particular certain existential notions regarding fertility and the life it propagates, which have a distinct feminine cast in contrast to sterility and death, which tend to be more associated with men.

These alignments do not, however, entirely lack ambiguity. Under certain conditions, pre-eminently in the cockfight, fertility can be indirectly associated with men (Cinatti 1987:146), a potentiality that elevates a mere pastime into an institution affecting the transformation of gender status. This metamorphosis plays on the contrast between the biological fact that whereas women are custodians of innate or biological fertility, men—if they are to contribute legitimately to the reproduction of the group—must somehow be made to acquire this capability. The cockfight, I shall argue, makes this acquisition possible.

Unmarried men impregnate women, of course, but their liaisons lack the ancestral endorsement that confers legitimacy on sex within marriage. Male fecundity as a biological potentiality remains, therefore, merely latent in a social sense, pending its confirmation in the person of a married male by the ancestors. Death and the bloodshed that attends it are the manifest tokens of this conversion of sexual potential into social potency. In contrast to cockfighting, in which men's reproductive powers are validated in bloodshed and death, kickfighting, although a violent sport performed by biologically potent males, suggests the social impotence of the unmarried male.

These distinctions help define the two modes of Tetum masculinity *(mane)*, which are nominally identified as *katuas* and *lawarik mane*. The former, as I mentioned earlier, denotes a married male, a socially complete male *(mane)* or "man." The latter denotes a bachelor, that is, a socially incomplete male or "boy." The feminine *(feto)* correspondents are *ferik* and *lawarik feto*.

Kickfighting: The Bloodless Sport of the Unmarried Male

Kickfighting is performed by bachelors, and its procedure lacks any preparation. A lad picks up its stratagems from watching more experienced exponents of the art and learns its techniques by casual practice with a like-minded partner. Exponents undergo no special training, and they generally compete in a friendly fashion, with no prizes being awarded or betting involved. The desire to engage in some form of socially acceptable violence and the pleasure of displaying one's agility before an admiring—and heterogeneously gendered—audience suffice as motives. They perform at any *ad hoc* gathering of neighbors.

The setting for a kickfight is as spontaneous as its character is simple. Any open patch of ground in view of men, women, and youngsters who assemble into an audience serves its purpose. The contestants perform barefooted and bare-chested wearing either a pair of shorts or a loincloth. They score hits with the inside of the foot, often as part of a basic attacking move consisting of a lunging swing made by either left foot or right foot directed at the side of the opponent's head or torso. Kicking straight out in reprisal or, more subtly, stepping sideways and away from the oncoming foot and countering with a kick oneself are the stock responses. Since his momentum diminishes if a lunge fails and encounters only the empty air, to maintain an onslaught an attacker must usually hop forward, rendering himself off-balance, and thus vulnerable to a counterstrike.

A contest begins as a pair of young men amble in an ostentatiously casual manner toward each other and square off in a sideways stance with their advancing feet (normally the left) pointing forward, their trailing feet directed away at right angles. The left hands hang at the side with fingers directed downward. Right-angled behind for balance is the other arm, the torso twisted back out of reach of a surprise kick. After holding this initial posture for several seconds the combatants circle each other, each poised on the balls of the feet trying to take advantage of an opening. Then, balancing on one leg and swaying backward a little, a boy will hop forward, in the manner just described, with his leading leg flexed to kick. Pausing a moment to gather his resources, he jumps forward again before swiftly straightening both legs as he attempts to deliver a kick with his leading foot. Using the hands offensively or defensively, or kicking below the navel, is prohibited. Occasionally a smothered attack may degenerate into a rough maul in which the rivals grapple with legs and arms. Prolonged mauling draws derisive hoots from the audience and these continue until the bachelors either disentangle their limbs or a senior man in the crowd tugs them apart.

The encounter ends when one contestant has scored a clean strike or after both score several hits and one or other contestant decides he has had enough. If a contestant falls, his opponent stands aside, permitting him to regain his feet, and at times even sportingly helping him. Before taking their leave, both winner and loser may preen themselves, thrusting out their chests and trilling like birds, their lively demeanor striking a contrast with the sullenness of some owners and bettors of a losing cock. Then, as spectators make way for them, the lads exit companionably, side by side.

Sometimes, following an imprudent lunge that has exposed him to a reprisal, a competitor is left no option but to take to his heels to avoid being kicked himself. Occasionally, he may find himself chased clean out of the ring of spectators who shout in delighted glee at the entertaining turn of events as they hastily jostle one another in getting out of the way. Unlike cockfighting, where a cowardly cock's wretched flight inflicts some humiliation on his owner, a bachelor who runs away—thereby submitting—does not diminish his self-esteem.

Cockfighting and the Blood of Men

Cockfights (see plate 7) usually accompany the Sunday markets held in Viqueque. Here the first of the four to ten contests that comprise a tournament begins early in the afternoon. By this time most of the morning's trading will have been concluded and wives, mothers, and sisters who have sold their family's agricultural produce will have handed over the money they have earned to their menfolk. The cockpit in Viqueque market is enclosed within a wooden stockade specially constructed for the purpose. At locations in the countryside a circle of spectators usually serves as the arena of combat, and as the fights progress the spectators maneuver around the frenzied maelstrom of feathers and claws to maintain a prudent distance from the flashing gaffs.

In some cockfighting traditions both legs of the cock bear a gaff, but on Timor this privilege falls to the left leg alone. Before a contest begins, the handler takes a length of thread of a red hue, and painstakingly attaches the flattened end of the gaff under the cock's natural spur or beside it. The double-edged three-inch weapon can be straight or sickle-shaped, and two-thirds of its length consists of a razor-sharp blade. The remaining one-third is flattened to fit the leg on which it is fastened tightly at an angle best suited to its wearer's style of combat. Some birds like to leap above an opponent with feet outstretched so that their strike comes downward. Some like to deliver a strike upward, from a crouch; some curve the trajectory of their strike; and some flail wildly away. A handler's tactical support can make all the difference to his cock's fortunes. This means he keeps continuing watch on the gaff, ever prepared to readjust its angle between rounds if he had originally misjudged the optimum angle or if the gaff has shifted position during the mayhem.

The action begins with each handler, cock raised in both hands at chest level, approaching the other. Birds whose demeanor lacks resolve are incited to anger by having their long tail feathers roughly jerked before being tossed summarily on the ground. Alternatively, the men may goad their cocks into pecking each other's combs. Once the fight has gotten underway a handler will respond to whatever sudden twist the fight may take. Should, for example, the contestants be stuck together or be "hung," the gaff of one impaling the other, the handler of the advantaged bird refrains from making a move. If his own cock has received a hit the handler deftly plunges into the fight (keeping hands and feet out of reach of the flailing gaffs) and tugs at the creature's tail feathers to extricate it, creating a respite for his bird. During such time-outs, a handler inspects his palpitating charge for any loss of blood, whatever dismay he shows eliciting shrilled delight from his rival's backers, the more exuberant of whom prance around trilling proudly like contestants during a kicking contest.

To revive his injured champion and reinstall whatever resolution he can summon, a handler will spruce up the comb, jowls, and flaps around the cock's ears or blow water into his mouth before he repositions it on the ground. One observer reported how a handler, in an attempt to "cleanse" his injured cock, plucked one of its tail feathers and stuck it down the bird's throat (Vondra 1968:72). Or, in a restorative attempt to replenish lost energy, a handler may rub the bird's back and thighs, stretch his legs, and blow into his open beak. Yet again, in the event the lung has suffered a rupture, he may resort to sucking blood from the bird's mouth. Blowing on the head is also held by some aficionados to be efficacious.

While the blowing into and upon the cock may be held to have a pragmatic restorative effect, the act itself has symbolic dimensions as well, since the Tetum associate life with breath *(kuis)*. In a tale recounted previously, we saw how an attempt was made to restore life to a corpse by blowing air down the length of a machete toward the corpse. Also, the image of life and fertility being blown into the bodies of the bride and bridegroom in the marriage ritual via betel and areca are evoked by a prayer at the marriage ritual (Duarte 1979: 393).

By employing the artifices described above, an experienced handler might keep a cock mobile enough to give him some hope of scoring a lucky hit during a protracted fight. Luck may be all a cock needs to turn defeat into victory, for even a crippled bird's gaff can maim or kill, and sudden reversals of fortune are common. In one fight I witnessed, a cock, too badly gaffed to do much more than wobble about on shaky limbs, had his beak taken into his handler's mouth. While the rival's handler scoffed and bettors pranced about trilling in anticipation of collecting their winnings, the man took the cock's beak into his mouth and blew water down the hapless bird's throat. Fortified to face what proved the final round, the stricken cock somehow managed to snag the other's body with its gaff, inflicting a lethal wound before it, too, expired.

Certain of the actions carried out by the handler—rubbing, blowing, and sucking—would seem excessive for the simple pragmatic goal of assisting his charge to make a kill. They are, however, consistent with several verbal and social facts that establish the common identity of man and beast. *Manu* is the Tetum term for "cock," but it is also slang for a man's penis, and the honorific title, *asu ua'in*, designates both a warrior who has succeeded in taking a head and a cock that has killed in the pit. As he approaches the cockpit, the owner of an especially prized cock proudly cradles "his alter-ego" (Cinatti 1987:146) in the crook of an arm, fondling, stroking, ruffling, and fluffing up his feathers.

Then, too, there is the analogy between the sexual restraint formerly imposed on a warrior who had taken a head and the treatment accorded a cock. Upon returning home a warrior would be segregated from the rest of his community and denied sexual access to his wife. Similarly, a champion cock is cloistered in a hole in the ground and segregated from his harem of hens, a few days before fighting.

Finally, many folktales include episodes in which the cock acts as metaphoric surrogate for his owner. In one example a prince in the guise of a cock clandestinely pays court to his lover whom he eventually impregnates. Scandalized, the woman's brothers murder her, but the prince miraculously restores her life. She subsequently gives birth to a boy who, years afterwards, when socially mature enough to have got a cock of his own, avenges his mother (Sá 1961:66–87). Another narrative recounts a king's personal rivalry with a prince. Their antagonism culminates in a cockfight in which each man wagers his life. After the prince's cock has slain its opponent, the prince then slays the king (Hicks 1990:104).

Given the fact that the cockfight is an exemplary institution of masculinity, it might seem something of a contradiction that it can be referred to by the expression *manu futu, manu hafeto malu*, "the cocks fight, the cocks [make] each other women." Ondina Fachel Leal's reflections on the gaucho cockfight are helpful as a starting point for an explanation. She contends that gaucho men identify with their cocks, who spill blood on their behalf, and states that they regard the natural world as the repository of certain important qualities deemed as admirable as they are desirable (Leal 1994:227–228):

> The intimacy [between cock and man], which is basically an exchange of attributes, is essential to the construction of maleness. Man acquires ownership over what he elects as animal nature, basically strength and power, and makes them part of human nature. This process of "naturalizing" certain attributes relies on previous and well-demarcated categories of what is nature and what is culture. Power in gaucho classification is part of nature; one way to obtain power is to have dominion over nature.

The Tetum work a variation of their own on the theme of acquiring control over a desirable property. However, they consider that men already possess power, so they have no need to seek this attribute What they do require is for their potential fecundity to be, as it were, "activated." The source of this validation is, as remarked earlier, the ancestors, and the authorization they confer in the cockfight is delivered through the medium of blood.[4]

Although in the past men shed blood in head-hunting, today they do so only when making sacrificial offerings to ancestors and to other sacred custodians of fecundity—as well as through their avian surrogates at cockfights. As an essential element of all sacrificial rituals, blood brings together human beings and ancestors, enabling the former to obtain fertility (Hicks 1996). By the ritual death of animals, whether chickens, pigs, or buffaloes, human life is reproduced and the community can perpetuate itself. Cockfighting permits men to conjure up ancestral validation for their sexuality by the blood their alter-egos shed on their behalf, and in so doing, like traditional head-hunting, this pastime functions as an instrument by which the violent shedding of blood activates the socially procreative potential of males. Once a male has matured enough to marry, his first cockfight confirms him as a reproductive force in society. Subsequent contests reconfirm his status.

Since their fecundity is perpetually active, premenopausal women do not have to sacrifice, take heads, or own cocks. Their involuntary and periodic shedding of blood is testimony enough of their fertility, and this quality, together with their faculty of giving life without taking it, makes female blood the quintessential symbol of reproductive power. Mary LeCron Foster (Foster 1979:182) reports a Balinese instance of the distinction between blood spilt in ritual violence and the nonviolent and nonritualized flow of menstrual blood:

> Male blood-spilling is an act of death, but has a redeeming, life-giving aspect that results from the climatic incorporation of betting and cock-eating. The reversal would seem to proclaim social or external creativity of men as opposed to the internal, biological creativity of women, a contrastive conceptualization in which female blood-retention is vital to procreative creativity and male blood-letting vital to social progress.

The Constitution of Gender

The procedure by which a male enters manhood commences at adolescence when his father presents him with a cock of his own to raise. The quiet informality of this occasion, which Cinatti characterizes as a rite of passage, and its privacy, belie its social significance (Cinatti 1987:146). Owning a cock that can be entered into competition is a sign of a male's developing maturity and shows he is ready for serious courtship. Oral literature underscores the importance of this period in a young man's life, and one common episode in folktales is a young bachelor leaving his natal home to embark on a journey, accompanied by his cock (Hicks 1990:104). As one *aiknananuk* puts it:

> The son goes away in a boat
> Taking with him his cock
> He goes alone with his cock
> His kin do not accompany him.

Several years must lapse, however, before society permits him to marry. Until he does, entering the cock in competition is considered unseemly, unless he has exceeded the time when he might have been expected to marry,[5] though this rule is often transgressed. Because manhood is considered only incipient until marriage confirms it, kickfighting offers the only socially acceptable public outlet for the violent impulses of an unmarried male.

The situation of a married man is of a piece with the character of cockfighting. Once married, a male is committed to socially influential and economically responsible roles that dictate a serious and purposeful attitude to life. Successful cockfighting, for its part, requires some measure of strategic forethought and preparation and has economic entailments. A bachelor's weaker social commitments, on the other hand, duplicate kickfighting's easygoing informality, which is a pastime lacking economic consequences. Sexually sterile in a sociological sense and jurally marginal, a man without a wife is authorized by the ancestral ghosts neither to fertilize a woman, and thus provide life, nor kill, via the agency of an animal surrogate. Marriage brings a young male to manhood by confirming him as a full kinsman in his father's descent group, the collectivity through which he gains access to his community's network of rights and duties. In former times, having assumed the obligation of providing his descent group with offspring, he would be required to undertake head-hunting expeditions in search of the bloody prize believed to possess the faculty of inducing the ancestors to bestow fertility on him and his wife. In his duplex role as ritually created provider of life and natural bringer of (fertility-inducing) death, a man *(katuas)* was set apart from bachelors *(lawarik mane)* and also from women *(ferik)* and girls *(lawarik feto)*.

In contrast to a married person, a bachelor, however biologically potent, is socially impotent since his sociological procreativity has yet to be confirmed by the ancestors. Thus his cock may not kill nor (in former times) could he shed blood in head-hunting. In this way, therefore, the cockfight not only delineates feminine values from masculine values, it makes it possible for two different forms of masculinity to be repeatedly dramatized in a public theater.

Comparable ideas occur elsewhere in eastern Indonesia. The Huaulu of Seram, to give only one instance, make a contrast between women's menstrual bleeding and the exclusive masculine prerogative to shed blood violently in cockfighting and head-hunting. As in Viqueque they construe the aggression implicit in Huaulu violence as an assertion of male control, but whereas the Tetum seek to make males as legitimately and omnipresently fertile as women, the Huaulu "[negate] menstruation, and thus femaleness, by the very act of *representing* it [emphasis in original]" (Valeri 1990:260).

Let us now reconsider the left leg and the gaff. Even aficionados of the sport in Caraubalo could not tell me why the gaff had to be affixed to this limb, but given the identify Tetum culture makes between the left side and death (Hicks 1984:93) it is logical that the local symbolism would assign the left limb as the leg wielding the lethal instrument. Less obvious, perhaps, is why the thread attaching the gaff to the leg should be red, which is the color of life and fertility (Hicks 1990:92). One possible explanation of this apparent contradiction is that the juxtaposition of life and death visually suggested here expresses the contradiction inherent in the ritual nature of the cockfight: the birds bring death to one another, yet by the death they inflict they also at the same time make it possible for the men they represent to bring life to the human community.

Sport affords the Tetum people a spectacular, as well as enjoyable, means of defining manhood, the total meaning of which is invested in a complex of ideas involving life, fertility, death, violence, blood, and ancestral jurisdiction. In so doing it signifies the ambivalence of indigenous gender classification, which is verbally condensed in the phrase "the cocks [make] each other women," for both the victor and vanquished (and their owners) are "feminized" by the spilling of blood. The bloodlessness of kickfighting, on the other hand, underscores the social impotence of its practitioners.

Studies of sport that represent it as an institutional expression of gender values typically do little more than reassert the sociological cliché that gender aligns with sport according to society's predominating classification of gender attributes. In this assertion masculine sports are assumed, in a straightforward correspondence of unambiguity, to define masculinity in contrast to feminine sports, which are held to define femininity. The pastimes of cockfighting and kickfighting in Caraubalo suggest that this is too constrained a perspective to impose on the capacity of sport to convey gender values. It suggests, to the contrary, that the enactment of gender-specific sports may actually conduce to what might be described as the "crossing-over" of basic gender properties. By disengaging the various indigenous constituents of masculinity, Tetum cockfighting and kickfighting demonstrate that so-called "masculine" sports do not invariably serve as paradigms for a monolithic definition of masculinity.

Endnotes

[1] When a marriage takes place between a man and a woman from the same clan the *na'an tolu* is not given. This is also the case when two men exchange sisters, a form of marriage called *feto tatuka*. Meat can be consumed in the marriage feast, but it will be contributed by both wife-giver and wife-taker who thus both share it.

[2] Although the Catholic Church was to become more of a presence in East Timor during the Indonesian interregnum than during the 1960s this mode of marital alliance remains (i.e., in the early twenty-first century) a vital institution in Timorese society, though one under some criticism by feminists and "progressives" who regard it as exploiting women.

[3] Alternative terms for "north" and "south" are *rae* and *lor*. The other pair of compass points lack gender associations. The east is *loro sa'e* ([the place where] the sun rises); west is *loro monu* ([the place where] the sun sets).

[4] Cocks are sometimes credited with supernatural attributes in narratives, where they behave much like ancestors. People gave conflicting opinions about whether or not in the cockfight the two competitors represent ancestors as well as the human owners of the cocks, but the possibility would be consistent with the motifs discussed here.

[5] If a man remains unmarried, which is unusual in this society, he is normally accepted as an active participant in cockfights only after he is well into his middle twenties, i.e., past the time when most males would normally be expected to have married.

Chapter 6

Kin and Ghosts

Reciprocal cooperation between kin and affines in either village attains its most elaborate expression upon the death of one of their members, and the ritual that is enacted is by far the most socially inclusive and well-attended collective gathering in the two villages. The immediate agent of death is the soul of the living individual. By permanently leaving its corporeal container it causes the latter to cease to function. The funerary ritual transforms this agent of death into an agency for creating life, namely, an ancestral ghost, by the collective authority of kin and affines who ritually combine to make it possible for this transformation to take place. This chapter describes the processes by which it is accomplished.[1]

Robert Hertz's (1907) study of the ritual responses made by societies to the death of a member abounds in analytical insights relevant to the mortuary ritual as performed today in Caraubalo, and those familiar with his famous essay will have no difficulty finding resonances in Tetum ethnography. He discerned very clearly as primary components of the ritual three entities: the corpse, the soul of the dead person, and the survivors. Hertz also remarked that the period that follows death is a time of danger for corpse and community alike. During this period, he argued, we find the body subject to a variety of rites designed to keep malign spiritual influences at bay and members of the community undergoing ritual treatments to serve the same end. Such themes are important defining elements of the Tetum death ritual, as formerly was his famous "secondary burial" or provisional burial, which proved anathema to Portuguese cultural sensibilities.

In Caraubalo the death ritual is known as the *tama mate* (*tama* = to enter, to bury). In the past, I was told, corpses were simply wrapped in a mat and eventually buried. Christians are interred in the cemetery *(rade)* of Santa Cruz, a place located near Barique, which is the *dato ua'in's* hamlet. Non-Christians are interred at a site near Baria Laran.

The form of the ritual I describe here is the most common I witnessed in Caraubalo, and the speeches are the standard ones. I was told that apart from a few differences, the rituals I attended were similar to those practiced three or four generations ago. However, three generations ago the corpse would be kept inside the house where it had lived and a smoky fire was lit under the house and under the corpse to dry it out. According to my informants, although the corpse stank, after the smoke had done its work members of the household could eat inside without having to suffer any unpleasant stench. Formerly also, there would be dances and songs at a woman's funeral, and when a king died the funeral would be considerably more elaborate, as happened with the death of perhaps the most prominent *liurai* in the subdistrict several years before my research, *Liurai* Paulo, of Uma Ua'in Craik *suku*. On that occasion drums were beaten and flags unfurled, and guests were expected to bring gifts of cloth *(tais)* and money.[2] There is a special set of terms used on the occasion of a *liurai's* death ritual, and these distinguish his social status from those of aristocrats and commoners. For example, the coffin that contains the body of a *liurai* as well as his death house are both known as *ro malai* or "foreign boat," a reference perhaps to certain myths that attribute foreign origins to *liurais*.

In actuality, death rituals are more haphazard spectacles than I describe here. A constant stream of visitors go to and from the deceased's hamlet: they assist at various tasks, leave for the night, and then perhaps return the next day. Parallel activities go on at the same time, even overlapping as a person leaves one task for a time to enter into another with the result that no two mortuary rituals are ever performed in quite the same way. However, after having participated in a number of funerals, I noticed that certain common procedures emerged from the apparent confusion, and individuals with whom I engaged in discussion were usually quite accurate in predicting the next turn a ritual was about to take. For all that, my findings are consistent with Robertson Smith's (1956/1889) suggestion that ritual behavior is prior to belief, since when they existed at all indigenous interpretations of what was going on were most often vague or even contradictory whereas ritual performances tended to be more consistent.

Ema Moris, Ema Mate

The most conspicuous feature of the funerary ritual is the role played by a group called *ema moris* or *ema banaka*. The term *ema moris* can be translated as the "people who [give] life," and *ema banaka* as "guests." The *ema moris* restore the gift of life to the close kin of the deceased person, and since this title conveys the group's primary and most vital function, I prefer to use it here. These close kin include all members of the hamlet where the death took place—the *knua mate*, "hamlet of death"— including the widowed person if the deceased was married and sundry other kin who, though residing in other hamlets, nevertheless wish to make a public demonstration of identifying with the deceased. These are the *ema mate* or the "people of death," who are linked with the world of the dead. They are less commonly spoken of as the *ema uma mate* or the "people of the house where the death has occurred."

The *ema mate* are aligned with the dead soul, and one from their group even attempts to prevent the departure of the corpse from the hamlet when it is time for it to be transported to the cemetery. Otherwise, during the course of the three days of ritual they are expected to maintain a low social profile and comport themselves passively. The *ema moris* function as enablers who restore the *ema mate* back to the human domain, and so they perform ritual actions upon the *ema mate* that suggest various kinds of severance or cleansing. They also remove the corpse from the community and—though it takes a year and three days to accomplish—dispatch the soul to the sacred world and facilitate its transformation into an ancestor. In performing this duty, the *ema moris* may be said to undergo something of a transformation themselves in that through a ritual reversal they—temporarily—identify with the ghosts of the *ema mate*, whom they evoke to participate in the ritual evacuation of the dead soul from the secular world.

Death

Babies who have died within a few days of birth and who have not yet received names are buried without ceremony in the wilderness. Although the final destination of an adult is the underworld there is some uncertainty about the fate of such children. People say they think the soul of a child goes "to talk with the sea, to play *(halimar)* with the sea," but their society's lack of a set of ideas regarding the destination of dead infants perhaps goes some way to explain why at their deaths a ritual barrier is erected to keep—or rather deflect—the dead soul away from the living community. Five days after the death of a boy and four days after that of a girl some coconut half-shells are placed outside the mother's hamlet at the conjunction of two paths. Bamboo ash from the mother's hearth is sprinkled inside each shell and placed on the ash is a leaf from the *fuka* shrub (*Calotropis gigantea*), to whose bark is attributed medicinal properties. Hand-spun cotton is put on top of the leaf, and every morning for the next seven days the mother visits the ritual ensemble, picks up each leaf in turn, and squirts out milk from her breasts onto it before returning the leaf to the ash. The ash symbolizes the hearth and the cotton symbolizes the infant's clothes. The leaf apparently merely serves as a container for the liquid. The purpose of this ritual is to deceive the dead soul, when it returns from the sea and wishes to revisit its mother at home to slake its thirst and warm itself in its clothes by the fire, into believing that the juncture where it encounters the ash and milk on the paths is in fact its home so it will venture no further. Were it to actually enter its former house the mother would fall ill. More half-shells may be added from time to time and the ash replenished with the milk and cotton as the need arises. Christians, such as Agostinha, tend to regard the ritual with skepticism.

A normal death, i.e., one that results from old age or sickness and not from accident, murder, or in childbirth, in most cases takes place in the sleeping area inside the house. The corpse is then placed on the front veranda and *ema moris* assemble to sing *mate lia*, the songs of death that I described in chapter 2, sometimes, in the case of a female corpse in former days, accompanying them with dancing. The songs may also be referred to by the more formal term *metan ho don* or "black and keening" (*metan* = black; *don* = keen).

Even while a person lies dying his or her closest kin (or, in the case of a wife, her husband's kin) choose two men to act as *maklaak manu ua'in* from their group so that immediately when death befalls they waste no time informing the residents of every Mane Hat and Mamulak hamlet of the death and inviting them to the funeral. This invitation is called the *ba katak ema mai mate* (to invite the people to the death [ritual]). In numerous ritual situations Tetum society prescribes that males and females be paired, the idea being to give tangible expression to the complementary roles they play in making life possible. So we find that in delivering this formal invitation the two *maklaak manu ua'in* are accompanied by a pair of women, whose job it is to issue a less formal invitation to the women of the hamlets visited.

Under traditional conventions a corpse could not be interred unless it had been viewed by the more important of its kin or relatives by marriage. When an eminent person died, for example the wife of a *liurai*, her kinship and affinal networks could be so extensive—perhaps covering most of East Timor—that it might be many years before the corpse could be buried. Today, this prescription is no longer in force because the law established by the Portuguese requires burial within three days.

The Invitation

When the emissaries arrive in a hamlet, a female elder steps forward to offer them lime, seven pieces of areca, and seven betel leaves in a basket. To do otherwise would be a ritual lapse, and the pair would return home. If that happened the offending hamlet would be penalized a goat or, perhaps, a chicken, which would be given to the hosts to atone for the mistake. After he has chewed betel, the head emissary addresses the woman who gives the offering in a speech replete with allusions to the social bonds connecting his kin with them and remarking on the ritual assistance the *ema mate* need in removing death from his community.

1. You lived here
2. You, our mother-in-law, Cassa Bo
3. The deceased used to come here many times
4. Seven of your daughters may perhaps visit us, too, and become pregnant[3]
5. Seven may provide us with descendants
6. But as yet your hand has not followed
7. But as yet your foot has not followed
8. Some water has been slopped
9. A little water has been spilt
10. It flows down to you, our affines
11. Whom we grasp, whom we hold tightly
12. Indeed you, mother-in-law, and we, are one person
13. In two persons
14. You, siblings-in-law, and we, are one person
15. In two persons
16. To whom we always give water
17. Who always address us in ritual words
18. Who rebuke us
19. The tree of the rat[4]
20. The rat in the tree
21. We don't like the death
22. We dislike it
23. But we shall cut the tree down
24. Run from the carrying basket
25. Until you arrive at the place of many houses
26. Until you arrive at the place of many midwives
27. Come to your sister
28. You, our mother
29. Our hand
30. Our foot
31. Come and listen
32. Come and join us
33. To find your eldest sister
34. You must leave your hamlet
35. But go no further
36. All your relatives, too, must come
37. All your senior males
38. They and their rebukes [to the dead soul] must come
39. You are our trouble [i.e., corpse and dead soul] removers

40. Regarding the corpse, the corpse
41. Force yourselves to see
42. Look at the tree
43. High! Its branches are high
44. Climb to place the coffin at its summit[5]
45. Climb its trunk *[kain]*
46. Change the dog, mother-in-law
47. Change the chicken, mother-in-law.

The emissaries then depart.

The tree mentioned in lines 42–45 is the tree in which the corpse traditionally would be placed before final burial in the ground. In the symbolism of Caraubalo it is identified with the tree in which the afterbirth is placed during the birth ritual (Hicks 1984:48). Here, the term *kain* (trunk, stalk) suggests the idea of a "link" or connection between death and birth. The tree is also identified with the clan tree, which itself is a symbol of the nexus between the individual and his clan ancestors (Hicks 1984:75). Lines 38–39 establish one justification for the death ritual, which is to remove the "trouble" plaguing the *ema mate*, that is removing the corpse, and by implication, removing the dead soul and the negative ritual condition of the *ema mate*, which is one of contamination through their intimacy with the deceased. The "rebukes" referred to are those that the *ema moris* will issue to the dead soul to urge it to leave the community and enter the sacred world when the corpse is about to be taken to the cemetery. In lines 46–47 the *ema moris* (represented by the mother-in-law) are urged to dispatch the corpse (dog) and dead soul (chicken) into the underworld. The water said to have slopped onto the ground, and the reference to flowing downhill (lines 8–10) presents an image of a stream flowing from the deceased's hamlet to that of the *ema moris*, and linking them. Line 16, "To whom we always give water," reinforces this image.

This image of water flowing downhill makes an appearance in the metaphorical language of the Northern Tetum (who practice the *fetosá-umane*, I might add). They liken the water that flows along the irrigation canals that surround and link different areas in a rice field with the life that women nurture and that is transmitted from wife-givers to wife-takers:

> The flow of the water is always from the source, going downstream, never upstream. In the case of connubial exchange, water symbolizes the woman. The *umamane* [wife-giving group] is the source or fountain of life by giving out its women. It is therefore called *ina-ama* (mother–father, parents). It is often called source, well, spring, virtue, strength of life, root and trunk of life, since it is the woman who conceives and bears children. The fact that brides come out from the *umamane*, makes the latter the source of life and children. (Brandewie and Asten 1976:21)

The "sister" (line 27) is any female the *ema moris* may ever have given in marriage to the dead person's hamlet, and line 33 specifies more exactly "eldest sister" because elder sisters generally marry before younger sisters. Thus they are said to be the "mothers" of the children who represent the future generations of the deceased's kin. The *ema moris* are beseeched to "run from" their hamlet (line 24) or "carrying basket" to that of the deceased's where they will find "many houses" (line 25) and "many midwives" (line 26). The large number of houses and midwives implies a fertile population with many offspring. The "hand" and "foot" (lines 6, 7, 29, 30) refer to the residents of the guest hamlet who are enjoined to come to the hamlet of the dead. Calling the female elder "Cassa Bo" (Cassa-the-Great) (line 2) evokes Cassa Sonek, the female source of Caraubalo's human *rai na'in* (aristocratic *[dato]*, landlord) population.

Funeral Preparations

The *ema moris* are, as I have said, responsible for the ritual and secular work that is involved with death in the hamlet. Nevertheless, as a practical matter, in order to start the proceedings, while the emissaries are travelling to the other hamlets, some *ema mate* of both sexes, who are not immediate kin of the deceased and who have already discharged their duty to keen in the presence of the corpse, will already have begun preparing the food. This activity includes crushing the corn and pounding the rice in long troughs and provides the first opportunity for men and women to sing *mate lia* together, with one person beginning a verse and his or her companions following suit. Singing lessens the drudgery somewhat, and when the rice has been pounded, they clean it on a large mat spread out on the floor.

Some male *ema mate* may begin the task of cutting down an Arenga palm and hollowing out its inside for the coffin. In former times the body would simply be wrapped in a mat and left on the front veranda of the deceased's house before being carried to the cemetery, placed in a tree, or deposited on a platform above the ground. Other male *ema mate* may gather bamboo for assembling the wall-less kitchen in which the food is to be prepared, and afterwards they slaughter pigs, goats, and buffaloes in preparation for the meals. Male *ema mate* may even begin to construct a pair of adjacent platforms about six feet above the ground, on one of which men cut up the meat and on the other women wash dirty dishes, plates, and cutlery. Other *ema mate* begin constructing the table and another wall-less building where they and the *ema moris* will eat after the body has been put in the grave. When they finish preparing the corn and rice they transfer the food from the mat to the kitchen. As food becomes available *ema moris* and hosts consume it on the various house verandas they have opted to sit on, with the *ema mate* helping themselves only after the *ema moris* have eaten.

When he arrives at the deceased's hamlet the leader of the group of *ema moris* from each hamlet hastens immediately to the *mate na'in* or "lord of death" and gives him two sets of gifts. The first is a contribution to the feast and consists of corn, rice, and a pig. The second gift is partly symbolic— "the four *patacas.*" It is a contribution to the bridewealth of the next male in the hamlet to marry, so he may engender a replacement for the deceased in due course. This theme is indicated in the speech made by the gift giver to the lord of death:

1. We are talking about [name of hamlet where death occurred]
2. We come about your female affines
3. Your mother
4. Noko Rubik
5. Nai Lekik
6. These words do not concern corn
7. They are not about rice
8. Instead, they concern Nai Lekik
9. Noko Rubik
10. [We] your affines
11. Those two who come to give you a new child
12. A fresh, green, child
13. But we have not forgotten your male kin
14. Your father
15. Funo Lekik
16. Leki Rubik
17. Your baby is below
18. There below
19. Go and seize it
20. Walk and seize it
21. Come, the banana's kinsmen
22. His father
23. Funo Lekik
24. Leki Rubik
25. Seize it again
26. Come, too, his female affines
27. His mother
28. Noko Rubik
29. The four of you
30. Your banana
31. Your boat
32. The white life is arriving
33. The red life is arriving
34. In its body
35. In its body
36. Seize and hold tightly
37. The *pataca lima nulu*

38. Your banana is coming
39. The earth is shaking
40. His kinsmen
41. His father
42. Funo Lekik
43. Leki Rubik
44. Seize it
45. Seize and hold tightly
46. The four patacas
47. Come and shake the ground more
48. The earth is shaking
49. Noko Rubik
50. Funo Lekik
51. The four of you
52. Now, look at your gifts
53. For you have listened to our words.

The phrases: "These words do not concern corn, they are not about rice," remind the lord of death that—although these staples are the food of life—the giver's statements are to be taken as metaphors. The "white life" (line 32) is the infant's soul; the "red life" (line 33) is its blood.

Boats are symbolically identified with, among other things, coffins. In past times, people would place the corpse of a king in a coffin that was termed "foreign boat," a designation also applied to the king's death house. Combined with an earlier inference concerning the Tetum view of human life, this association provides us with one possible interpretation of the reference to "boat" (line 31). By creating a parallel between "banana" and "coffin," this line and line 30 may be intended as an elliptical statement as to the cyclical pattern of existence, that is, emergence (as a banana) from the earth, and a return to the place in the coffin at death.

The female figures, Noko Rubik and Nai Lekik (lines 4, 5, 8, 9, 28, 49), are names that stand for the *ema moris*. Their male complements, Funo Lekik and Leki Rubik (lines 15, 16, 23, 24, 42, 43, 50), are names that stand for the *ema mate*. The relationship terms mother (lines 3, 27) and female affines (lines 2, 26), like Noko Rubik and Nai Lekik, symbolize the *ema moris* as representing all lineages related as affines to the deceased's group; the terms father (lines 14, 22, 41) and male kin (line 13), and Funo Lekik and Leki Rubik, symbolize the *ema mate*.

Line 11 underscores one purpose of the encounter. The *ema moris*, as affines, come "to give . . . a new child" to the *ema mate*. For their part the *ema moris* are commissioned to install the dead in the world of the sacred and encourage a baby to emerge from it into the material world. The *ema mate* are urged to seize the "banana" (lines 19, 20, 25, 36, 44, 45), *pataca lima nulu* (line 37), the four *patacas* (line 46), and baby (line 17), which have been given by the *ema moris*. The infant, nevertheless, is recognized as the joint creation of the two descent groups, so on line 13 comes the reminder that the creative role of the *ema mate* has not been "forgotten." The references to "earth" and "ground" (lines 39, 47, 48) accord with the cycle of life motif. As is literally the case with the banana, but only figuratively with the *pataca lima nulu*, the infant emerges from the "ground," or mother goddess "earth," who is said to shake like a human woman giving birth. The infant must be "seized," "held tightly" (lines 19, 20, 25, 36, 44, 45) as it comes up from "below" (lines 17, 18).

The *ema mate* stop their work when the *ema moris* begin to arrive in the hamlet of death. Henceforth for the remainder of the death ritual the *ema mate* remain unobtrusive while the *ema moris* dominate the scene. Before taking over, however, the *ema moris* must pay their respects to the deceased and his or her family. They accordingly form a line to view the corpse and perhaps keen as soon as they enter the hamlet. This at least is the convention. In practice few men actually do so, and keening is left to the women who accompany them. The junior men and women begin the various chores they are responsible for, taking over from the *ema mate*. Meanwhile senior men go off by themselves to various houses where they sit on the front verandas to talk, chew betel, drink, and perhaps play cards with elders who arrived before them. When they sit down women of the hamlet offer them the ingredients for betel-chewing in the customary baskets in which betel-chew is offered to *ema moris*. Later, senior women *ema moris* who wish a respite from keening sit apart from the men on the lateral verandas of the houses.

When they enter the hamlet of death the *ema moris* also give culinary utensils such as dishes, plates, and cutlery for the communal meal that ends the funeral to the aforementioned lord of death *(mate na'in)* who is in charge of the three-day ritual. He is chosen by the hamlet and is often its senior elder. The lord of death notes who gives what utensils, for these are loaned items.

There are specific gifts expected from kin. A grandson gives one buffalo upon the death of a grandfather or a grandmother. A man gives one buffalo or pig and a piece of masculine cloth when his father dies. Upon the death of his mother he gives one buffalo or pig, and a piece of feminine cloth. When his wife's father or mother dies he gives a pig, a piece of masculine cloth, rice, and four cans of fish to "remember the widowed person." When a mother's brother or his wife dies, the gift consists of one pig, one piece of cloth, or the cash equivalent. When a son-in-law or daughter-in-law dies, the gift amounts to a pig and a masculine cloth.

The lord of death places whatever money he has been given in a basket standing on the sacred shelf of the dead person's house. Later, when the commensal meal has been consumed, the money becomes the property of the widowed person, or, if the deceased himself were already widowed, of the eldest son (or daughter), who may use it as he (or she) desires.

Female *ema moris* wrap a white cloth—not a dark color as would signify death, but the color of life, as a reminder that life emerges from death—around the coffin after it has been placed in the death house. When this has been done, men tack nails into the cloth at either end of the coffin, each set so that when red and yellow threads are wound around the nails they form a star-like shape the villagers liken to the sun. In more traditional times, people claimed, only royalty was allowed to display this emblem, but today it is in common use.

Meanwhile, other *ema moris* cut the hair of some of the women most closely related to the deceased, a rite of separation carried out on the verandas of the houses owned by the *ema mate*. In another separation rite, *ema moris* remove the corpse's clothes, wash the corpse, and destroy the deceased's weapons, eating plate, drinking mug, and other personal effects. However, the dead person's personal pouch *(kohe mate)*, which once held the deceased's betel-chew when he or she was alive, is filled with fresh betel-chew and hung up in the dead person's house near the pouch dedicated to the ghosts. The *kohe mate* provides a place of rest and the betel-chew that is deposited inside provides nourishment for the dead soul over the course of the three days, for if the soul is hungry it is a prudent move to cater to its needs. The same sacrifice is made to the ancestors of the household, because they, too, will be visiting the house and must not be allowed to find fault with the way they are being treated. The *ema moris* then dress the corpse in one or more cloths, called the *tais mate* or "clothing of the dead."

Still other *ema moris* erect the death house. Until the death house has been constructed and the coffin filled, the hamlet of death is a hive of activity. Thereafter only the cooks remain at work.

The Death House

As opportunity permits, the *ema mate* and the *ema moris* take temporary time off from their labors to keen in the house where the death occurred, and after the corpse has been transferred, they continue their display of ritual anguish later inside the death house. There, women and men (though the former predominate) maintain their stylized wailing for hours at a stretch until the coffin is finally carried away. The death house is usually about eighteen feet long and several yards wide, and it is raised three or four feet above the ground on wood piles. The entrance is at the front, and to the right, as one looks at the entrance, is its exit. If the deceased were Christian, somewhere in the house religious pictures and perhaps a rosary dangle from one of the beams.

Death houses are fairly standard in construction except for their frontal verandas, which vary in depth and accordingly accommodate fewer or more senior mourners who congregate on them to talk after

completing any keening they may have done. When the death house is
ready and the coffin inside awaits its occupant, males of the *ema moris*
carry the corpse in a mat to the building. They cover the corpse's face
with a white handkerchief, signifying life. Once the body is inside the
coffin the men nail the lid down, discard the mat in the woods, and
wash their hands in warm water heated in a pitcher standing on a special hearth constructed for just this purpose and physically set apart
from the hearth used for preparing food. The widowed person and
other *ema mate* most closely akin to the deceased are escorted by *ema
moris* to the death house to continue their keening there.

For both corpse and *ema mate* the transition period between death
and life extends over three days. Inside the death house the corpse
lies undisturbed while around it on all sides the widowed person, parents, siblings, and children kneel side by side, heads covered with
black cloths, and arms around one another's shoulders, keening and
chanting *mate lia*. From time to time an impassioned keener will sway
forward until her or his head touches the coffin before straightening
up, and from time to time *ema moris* who have recently arrived will
quietly enter the building and start keening at whichever vacant place
around the coffin they can find. When their obligation is concluded
they leave to eat or sit on the veranda. For the two nights the funeral
dirge can be so loud as to make sleep difficult, even for persons in
neighboring hamlets, and some mourners go the best part of three
days without sleep.

I was told that in the past *ema mate* and *ema moris* alike would chew
betel in the death house at the same time, "as a single unit," in a ritual
whose intent was to underscore the association of womanhood with
fertility. A woman would address first the female elders and then the
male elders who were present. With both arms crossed and her two
sets of fingers under her armpits, the woman would address her female
colleagues in the following words:

1. Lady wife of the *makair fukun*
2. Lady wife of the *dato ua'in*
3. Also your elder sisters present
4. Also your younger sisters present
5. You who are elders of the wife-taking groups
6. You who are elders of the wife-giving groups
7. Who shade us from the sun
8. And talk with us
9. You, many elders
10. Chew betel!

She would then offer them areca, betel, and lime for betel-chewing,
from a basket.

Next the woman would direct the following speech to the male elders:

1. Lord *makair fukun*
2. Lord *dato ua'in*
3. Also your elder brothers present
4. Also your younger brothers present
5. You who are elders of the wife-taking groups
6. You who are elders of the wife-giving groups
7. Who shade us from the sun
8. And talk with us
9. You, many elders
10. Chew betel!

Then they, too, would be offered the ingredients for betel-chewing.

At noon on the third day when everyone has had a chance to keen and the grave has been dug, senior male *ema moris* command a group of about eighteen unmarried men to carry a bamboo litter to the death house.

The task of dispatching the corpse to the afterlife is far from smooth, for the dead soul desires to remain among its living kin. As one *mate lia* phrases it:

They launch the boat on the sea
The boat does not go
They push the boat into the sea
The boat does not go
The boat is secured with a weight
The boat is secured with a rope.

The bachelors stand holding the litter at right angles to the house; half of them holding one side, half holding the other. When they have taken a firm grasp they begin swaying rhythmically and in unison from side to side. This movement is known by three names. First, and most commonly used, is *lossu bessi* (*lossu* = to open; *bessi* = strongly), "to open strongly": to open the body and impel the dead soul into leaving. The soul leaves the body at death and may try to re-enter its former receptacle, in this way returning it to "life." *Lossu bessi* is delivered as a threat of violence towards a dead soul should it try to recapture the body. The second term, *tate andar*, "to soothe the stretcher," is more conciliatory; while the third is lyrical—indeed hopeful—*foti manu bikia* (*foti* = to elevate; *bikia* = to distress), "to elevate the distressed bird." The dead soul, here, is likened to a saddened bird flying up out of the corpse to gain happiness in the other world.

As they gently rock the litter the bachelors inform the soul that they no longer regard it as human. It has no kin. They request their ghosts to convey the soul to the world of the sacred as they themselves will shortly be conducting its physical remains to the grave in the forest:

1. You poor, poor orphan
2. You poor one, your mother is not here
3. Your father is not here
4. Your mother no longer exists
5. Your father no longer exists
6. We are very near burying you
7. In the cemetery of Santa Cruz
8. Ghosts
9. Ancestors, come
10. Walk near us
11. Approach us
12. Enter our door.

While the recitation proceeds, two unmarried female *ema moris* each put on a sarong, more colorful than their usual apparel, an embroidered blouse, a bracelet, earrings, hairpins, and a head cloth. Two women help them, and all four stand on a mat. While preparing themselves, the girls step off the mat only to have their feet washed in a bowl of water. When the two girls have dressed, they are joined by two young men dressed in traditional fashion as warriors. In his left hand, each warrior grasps a spear, and in his right, a war sword, weapons signifying the protective power of the *ema moris* against any onslaughts initiated by the dead soul. As they do so, the litter bearers clamber into the death house, and from it they lift the coffin, which they bring outside and place on the ground. There, in front of the house, they attach the casket firmly to the litter with stout cords.

Every *ema mate* hastens to the front of the death house, where the widowed person is kneeling at the feet of one of the warriors. If it is a woman, she puts her arms around his feet, and rests her forehead on the ground, careful not to touch his legs with her head or hands, and pleads that her husband be allowed to remain with her and his kinsfolk. Rising, she repeats her plea at the second warrior's feet. Both ignore her, and move to the front of the house and once there perform an action in which, shoulder to shoulder, the boys shuffle forward and backwards, right feet leading, twisting their weapons about with short movements of their forearms. After a minute or so they shuffle up to the coffin, which they gently touch at a point over the corpse's head with the tips of their swords and spears, as though to tap the dead soul from the corpse's head should it have taken up lodging there. They shuffle back and return six more times, after which they advance in a normal manner towards the coffin as though to carry it off to the grave. They reach it and as if on cue a tremendous cry erupts from somewhere in the depths of the death house. Brandishing his own sword high in the air, the lord of death, apparently galvanized into action, leaps onto the front veranda, in a ritualized attempt to keep the corpse among its kin.

Undeterred by his dramatic appearance the two warriors advance resolutely towards the lord of death, full of purpose, their swords and spears thrust forward in a counteroffense. In ritual verse they recite that the soul has been strongly forced out of the community, adding that death has fractured the integrity of the hamlet, and that despite his reluctance to permit the corpse to be taken away, the lord of death, too, must endorse their determination to remove the dead soul from the community:

1. We have beaten it strongly
2. We have beaten it strongly
3. It has departed
4. The hamlet group is broken
5. [But still] The corpse is forcing us to [repeat] these words
6. [And] even you must speak them
7. These words must come
8. You have to utter them loudly
9. They must be uttered forcefully
10. We have beaten it strongly
11. We have beaten it strongly.

The warriors return to their starting position, and the lord of death joins his fellow *ema mate*. To the accompaniment of raucous shouting by all, the coffin bearers hoist up the litter, and make a move for the cemetery, pointing the corpse's feet towards this destination. The other *ema moris* begin to enter the forest after them. But just before they clear the confines of the hamlet, the widow and a few other *ema mate* make one final attempt to prevent the deceased from leaving. They shove themselves past the bachelors and rest their hands on the coffin. For a few moments the bachelors tolerate this, but then resume their interrupted departure and physically remove the corpse from the hamlet. Their route to the cemetery must not pass near any other hamlets, for these are "hamlets of life" (*knua moris*).

Holding a small tray of flowers covered with a white cloth, the aforementioned girls lead the mortuary cortège as it wends its way through the forest, the corpse's feet directed towards the cemetery. From the left wrist of each girl dangles a *kohe mate* (the pouch of death), and from the right wrist a *kohe moris* (the pouch of life). Inside both are the ingredients for betel-chew.

Immediately behind the two girls in the cortège come the two warriors. Next comes the coffin, and bringing up the rear the rest of the participants in the ritual. The journey to the cemetery is punctuated by the opposing sets of coffin bearers tussling with one another seven times. The bearers on one side of the litter represent the force of the dead soul and the ones on the opposite side represent humanity. Each time humanity triumphs as its rivals sprawl on the ground. These scuffles are called the *dun malu* (*dun* = to banish, to separate, to intimidate; *malu* = each other): "to separate one from the other." Were the dead soul to succeed in overpowering the coffin bearers the soul would be able to pry open the coffin lid and reunite with the corpse. After each tussle the coffin bearers continue on their way until the next struggle. The seventh tussle ends just outside the entrance to the cemetery and marks the soul's acquiescence in the loss of its former body.

The corpse's final journey, from hamlet to grave, parallels the journey of the dead soul to the land of the dead described in many Timorese narratives (Hicks 1988) and the boat mentioned in such stories identifies with the coffin, an identification consistent with the courtesy language used to refer to royalty, where the expression "to carry the coffin of a king" is rendered as *dudu ró malai* or, literally, "to push the boat out to a foreign land." The prominence of the two girls in the funeral cortège asserts this association, for in Timorese poetry the boat is identified with womanhood (Duarte 1979:381) and draws attention to the role of females in mediating between the world of the living and the world of the dead.

At the graveside the bachelors place the coffin on some wide teak leaves that adorn flat stones near the opening to the grave, its "vagina," whose depths are referred to as *rai lolon* or the "womb of the earth." The actual burial itself is called by the same term as the mortuary ritual itself, *tama mate*. To prevent the earth from touching the coffin, a piece of cloth, the *hena laka* (*laka* = to shine) lines the bottom of the pit. The bachelors, and any male who can get a grip on the supporting ropes, lower the casket to the bottom. As the coffin is being lowered into the grave, the girls drop their two pouches of death on the coffin while the other *ema moris* distribute the contents of the two pouches of life among themselves as they cluster around the graveside. When the casket settles on the cloth, a man jumps down to wrap the ends of the cloth over the coffin top. He next fastens them together with large pins, and finally places a black cloth over it.

When a Catholic is buried his or her body is aligned so that the head points to the west and the feet point to the east, "because they follow what the priests tell them." For a non-Christian the head points to the east and the feet point to the west, which is the land of the ancestors when the underworld is represented in the horizontal plane rather than in the vertical.

The warriors stand on guard lest the soul launch an onslaught against the mourners who each toss a clod of earth onto the coffin. Then when men fill the grave in, the two girls lay the flowers they have been holding at the head of the grave. If the deceased were not a Catholic the two warriors, standing at the head of the grave, recite the following verse:

1. His head has become white
2. His leg has become white
3. His head is buried
4. But his leg remains out
5. His leg is buried
6. But his head remains out
7. Tomorrow
8. His head will be laid to rest
9. His leg will be laid to rest.

The first six lines betray the unease of the villagers regarding the dead person's corpse, which has now been incorporated into the earth womb *(rai lolon)*. Yet his invisible (or "white") soul may be anywhere. Lines 3–6 make the contrast between the corpse's clear-cut status in the underworld and the uncertainty villagers feel about the status of the soul. Only the *keta mate*, which will transform the dead soul into an ancestral ghost, will decisively set their minds to rest. But that ritual valediction is still a year away ("tomorrow," line 7).

Here is a tale that gives us some idea of the unsettling feelings some of the more suggestive mourners claim to experience on these occasions:

Two brothers lived together. A kinsman died. They decided to keen over his corpse. The younger brother was frightened; the elder was not. The coward sat far from the body. The brave brother sat very near. Having no fire the elder ordered his younger brother to go out for a firebrand. After the coward had left, the brave brother grabbed the corpse and made it a pillow for his head. With his head on the cold pillow he dropped off to sleep.

The younger brother had meanwhile met a boy carrying a firebrand. He seized it. Returning home his first words were, "Oh! I'm so frightened of the corpse!" His elder brother replied, "All right! Fetch it here!" The coward said, "I can't. I'm too frightened!" The brave brother stalked over to him, snatched the firebrand, and clambered up the stairs into the "womb" of the house where the corpse lay. But just as he was staring into the dead face he suddenly, to his horror, saw the corpse come back to life. The coward screamed in terror, but his elder brother quickly regained his nerve. The corpse then began to get up. Jumping down the stairs, the coward rushed out of the hamlet and ran for a hill. He certainly was a coward! His brother ran from the house more slowly. He was a bad sprinter, and the corpse began catching up with him.

The brave brother ran to the tall tree in which the coward was hiding and started climbing it. It was tough work. The corpse reached the foot of the tree and shouted up, "All your talking revived me. I can now walk. Come down!" "Oh!" replied the coward, "I'm too scared to come down." "You can't stay up there forever," mocked the corpse. "Your brother should have made sure my soul was safely in

the sacred world before fooling around with me." Then, taking hold
of the tree it shook the branches until the coward was thrown down.
The corpse grabbed him. Then it shook the tree a second time, and
down fell the elder brother. And so the two brothers died.

Then, while the pair of warriors remain standing guard against the
dead soul, the mourners leave the cemetery. When the burial is over the
girls take the two pouches of life to the hamlet where the deceased had
passed away. Both are filled with the ingredients for betel-chew, and one
pouch is hung from a beam in the death house, its presence suggesting the
complementarity of life and death. The other pouch is hung in the
deceased's bedroom, on a main beam. Its title is *mate bein nia kohe*, "the
pouch of the ghost," a designation anticipating the dead soul's attainment
of this status. The dead soul is characterized as purely malevolent, but it is
a token of hope that when the dead soul takes to wandering around the
hamlet it will be too eager to devour the gifts inside to trouble its kin. The
name also hints that life will overcome death, for it is the ancestors, not
the dead soul, who are the source of life.

In the days to come when the flowers that were placed on the grave
by the two girls eventually wither, the girls replace them. Then with the
decay of the second bunch, a third and final posy is placed on the grave.
When these flowers, too, have withered, men formerly of the category of
ema moris raze the death house to the ground, and destroy its contents,
including the pouch of life. From the time the corpse is interred to the
time this building is destroyed, only the two flower-carrying spinsters will
have entered it, when they hang the pouch of life inside.

After the rite of commensality that reintegrates the *ema mate* into secular existence, this designation and that of *ema moris* are dropped. To dra-
matize this reincorporation, a ritual reversal takes place. Whereas the *ema
moris* have hitherto served meals to the *ema mate*, the *ema mate* now serve
this final meal to the *ema moris*.

Dead souls are normally invisible, but I was told that if one uses a
mirror when in the presence of a soul one can actually glimpse its spectral
form quickly passing to and fro across the mirror's surface. When seen in
this way, the soul, which is said to appear in human form, though of vari-
able dimensions, is of a white color.

One year after the interment the *keta mate* (to cut away the dead) completes the set of ritual acts that makes up the mortuary ritual. The black
armbands that Christians wear are cut off (*keta metan* = to cut off the
black), and Catholics and non-Christians alike celebrate for anywhere up
to three days the final incorporation of the soul into the sacred world. The
keta mate, as I have earlier remarked, makes the dead soul a ghost, an
event joyously celebrated with plenty of pork and goat meat, washed
down with wine. The speech that was recited at the graveside during the

deceased's burial is repeated, and to ritually affirm the severance *(keta)* of the soul from the material world, the former *ema moris* smash the deceased's sacred jar, bamboo drinking cup, and spoon. They also crunch up the pouch of life that had been hung in the deceased's house and discard its pieces into the wilderness immediately adjacent to the hamlet where the death occurred, and at the point where one of the paths leading from the hamlet into the wilderness bisects. This location, of course, replicates that selected when a baby dies and its mother places the half coconut shells on the ground. The detritus is henceforth regarded as *lulik* and therefore dangerous to touch. Only the passage of time and the agencies of sun and rain eventually remove it from sight when they join forces to incorporate it into the earth, there to join the corpse. Before the Portuguese imposed their three-day law, up to nine years might lapse before a *keta mate* would take place. Then the possessions of several deceased individuals who had died over the years intervening since their burial would be destroyed in a general *keta mate*.

The Redemptive Authority of Death

Émile Durkheim underestimated the reciprocal character of the relationship that could exist between sacred and secular, a reciprocity that in Tetum cosmology emerges as a necessity in which ghosts and kin depend upon each other. Once its sacred element—the soul—has permanently evacuated the body, the body can no longer function dynamically in the secular world and must be delivered to the world of the dead. The same, however, is true for the sacred force, the soul, the vital agency animating that body. Once bereft of its material container the dead soul can no longer survive in the material world, but must be dispatched, with the aid of its ancestral ghosts, to their world where it is transformed into an ancestor itself, there to receive sustenance in the form of regular sacrifices from its human kin.

This world of death is also the world of life. I have sought to demonstrate that Tetum ritual behavior implies that the spirits possess the authority to confer fertility, and through this capacity provide human beings with the means of sustaining life, but as we have seen they also have the power to bring about infertility and the eventual extinction of the descent group. Implicit, therefore, in death is life, a paradox visually recalled by the two unmarried girls, who represent fertility, carrying the two pouches of life with them as they lead their dead colleague on his or her last journey to the grave.

Infertility is the antipode of fertility, and in no context is this more apparent than in that of death, which may be regarded as infertility at its most uncompromising, a factor that may help explain the prominence of the death ritual in Caraubalo Tetum society. As I have remarked earlier, the household is the focal social unit, and lineages and even more, clans, have become less relevant in the lives of the villagers. In 1966–1967 the death ritual and the marriage ritual were the most inclusive institutions for providing the system of descent groups with high visibility and effectiveness, but of the two, the former was decidedly more prominent.

The funerary ritual, as already noted, is also the most complex of the Tetum rituals. Ritual, in one definitional sense, may be regarded as order put to purposive, symbolic effect. By the authority it commands, Tetum ritual equips its participants to summon up the creative powers of the spirits who, if they accept this commission, will bring abundance to humanity. On the other hand, human disregard of proper behavior invites ghostly retribution (the sacred no longer remains "set apart" *[keta mate]* in the Durkheimian sense) as the residents of Bua Laran discovered when they displeased their ancestors (see chapter 4). Unrestrained by ritual, the ghosts seize the initiative, which means they are free to inflict whatever punishments they choose; so destruction overcomes the promise of creation; infertility replaces fertility; and death overwhelms life. Symbols of this retribution—corpses, dead souls, the kin of the deceased—visually place these negative aspects of existence on display where every member of the community can see and reflect upon them. Furthermore, participation in the ritual instructs the villagers in the knowledge that their mortuary ritual offers the only means of nullifying the destructive consequences of death. Each performance reinforces this truth. The residents are present when the corpse is disposed of in the grave; the people of death are reinstated in the world of the living; and the dead soul is—though the process takes a year and three days—installed in the sacred world, the domain of the dead but simultaneously the source of life.[6]

This idea of conjoining death and the source of life is ritualized in another East Timorese population residing along the north shore, not far from the border with West Timor, where lies a lagoon called Bemalai (Hicks 1996). Before the Indonesian occupation there used to take place at this sacred site an annual ritual performed towards the end of the dry season when plant life was withering and animal life was experiencing a debilitating lack of vitality. In this ritual the local king would be slain symbolically, and his soul dispatched to the sacred world and brought back. His soul's restoration to the body restored not only the leader of his community to life but also replenished the natural resources of the secular world. Like the Bemalai ritual, the Caraubalo funerary ritual demonstrates in a vivid manner to its participants that life derives from death and that humanity depends on the spirits it has invented for the perpetuation of life. A dead soul becomes a ghost; an agent of death becomes an agency for life-affirming fertility; and kin become ghosts.

Endnotes

[1] The description given here incorporates ethnographic data first included in *A Maternal Religion*, where, however, the death ritual is presented in terms of the model propounded by Arnold van Gennep.

[2] Thirty years or so after my first period of research in Viqueque his son, *Liurai* Miguel da Costa Soares, received the same sort of spectacular funeral, and I was later able to see a videotape of it in the house of his daughter, Maria Rosa da Costa Soares, in Darwin, Australia.

[3] The Tetum text literally says "carry the root"; "the root" is a metaphor for the line of descent.

[4] This is Arenga palm, the tree from which coffins are made.

[5] It is said that formerly the corpse could also be temporarily placed on a tall platform.

[6] The ritual association of life and death is common in certain societies. Among the Merina, of Madagascar, for example, "taking part in the [funerary] ceremony . . . helps towards fertility and, in particular, fighting for the mats in which the bodies have been wrapped is seen as a direct aid to fertility" and "it is the dead who have been and will be the suppliers of life" Bloch (1971:221–22). As Maurice Bloch and Jonathan Parry 1982:41) phrase it, ritual supplies an "alchemy which transforms death into fertility."

Pl. 1. Caraubalo Basin, as seen from Baria Laran and looking northward towards a gap in the mountainous backbone of eastern Timor. The coconut trees, savanna, and bamboo-fenced garden are typical of the Basin.

Pl. 2. A small herd of buffalos on the road from Viqueque town to Uato Lari *Posto*.

Pl. 3. The stone slab that forms the base for the geode or mother stone (*fatuk kabua*): view from several yards taken in the region of Vessa village, Caraubalo *suku*.

Pl. 4. A close-up of the same altar. Inside the concave cavity one may see the fragments of stone ("children") the mother stone (*fatuk kabua*) is said to have given birth to.

Pl. 5. Four lads threshing dry rice in Mamulak.

Pl. 6. The Uma Kik *suku* chief, Miguel Soares, in ceremonial garb. Before the Portuguese imposed a firm colonial hand on Timor such chiefs would lead their warriors on head-hunting forays outfitted like this. In Miguel Soares' hand is a ritual sword (*surik*), on his head a golden ornament shaped like a buffalo horn (*kaibouk*), and on his chest a golden disk (*belak*). His wristwatch is material evidence of acculturation.

Pl. 7. José Pereira watching a pair of cocks sparring.

Pl. 8. Nai Lequi Agostinha and Lihu Lequi, welcoming the *ema banaka* into Rubi Loik's house where his body lies before it is transferred to its death house. They will keen as soon as they enter the house. This was not the Rubi Loik who was one of my major sources of information.

Pl. 9. The "people who give life" bring their gift of corn to Dau Bua Mahan on the occasion of the death ritual for Rubi Loik. Rubi Fonok (José), son of Funo Rubik (Caibowki lineage), unpacks the corn from the back of the packhorse.

Pl. 10. Four *ema moris* split the trunk of a palm to make the lid of the coffin for Rubi Loik.

Pl. 11. Dau Caik, the one-year-old daughter of Cai Rubik and Hare Rubik, residents of the hamlet of Manu U'e Matan, died after falling off the veranda of her parents' house. Here we see men hollowing out a palm to make her coffin.

Pl. 12. *Ema moris* building a house in which "people who give life" and "people of death" will eat the funeral feast for Dau Caik.

Pl. 13. Young men in a moment of levity at Dau Caik's funeral larking about
with the table top they are constructing for the death ritual feast.

Pl. 14. A mortar in which corn and rice are pounded on communal occasions. The two poles attached to the mortar enable men to carry it. In the background is the table upon which the funeral meal for Dau Caik will later be eaten. The author sits in the background.

Pl. 15. Men singing songs of death (*mate lia*) for Dau Caik as they pound the grain in their mortar.

Pl. 16. Women singing death songs for Dau Caik as they pound rice in their mortar.

Pl. 17. The *tate andar:* Dau Caik's coffin bearers singing her songs of death before moving to the death house with their litter to pick up the coffin and remove it to the cemetery.

Pl. 18. The *tate andar*: men singing death songs with the stretcher on which Dau Caik's coffin will be transported to the cemetery. The *makair fukun* can be seen on the left immediately behind the line of litter-bearers with his right hand on his hip.

Pl. 19. Dau Caik's coffin about to be taken from a hamlet and carried to the cemetery.

Pl. 20. The dead child's female kin keening around Dau Caik's coffin before it is taken to the cemetery.

Pl. 21. The two women, one of whom is Nai Lequi Agostinha (right) ritually dress the two funeral procession leaders before Dau Caik's ritual procession.

Pl. 22. Nai Lequi Agostinha (left) overseeing one of the two funeral procession leaders ritually wash her feet before Dau Caik's funeral procession.

Pl. 23. At Dau Caik's funeral Nai Lequi Agostinha ritually dressing one of the two girls who will lead the funeral procession to the cemetery.

Chapter 7

Retrospect

Here I shall take the opportunity hindsight affords of casting a quick glance over the last quarter century and provide a retrospective summary of what befell the people of Timor after my departure in 1967.

In Viqueque, as elsewhere in Portuguese Timor, social change proceeded imperceptibly for the next seven years, but then in complete contrast with the sleepy routine of daily life political events unfurled with a ferocity that overwhelmed the population. On 25 April 1974 the political regime that had governed Portugal for decades was overthrown in a left-wing coup, the leaders of which hastily committed themselves to divesting the mother country of its colonies. This included, of course, the political backwater that for centuries had been Portuguese Timor, which was offered three choices: the Timorese could choose to have some sort of federated autonomy under Portugal; they could have independence, either as part of a member of a Portuguese commonwealth or not; or they could choose integration into their giant neighbor, the Republic of Indonesia, the leaders of which were only too anxious to make Portuguese Timor an Indonesian province.

The Portuguese government decided the choice should be made known by means of a plebiscite in which all Timorese adults would vote their choice, an ambition that betrayed its leaders' ignorance of the colony. In 1974 Portuguese Timor's population was roughly 646,155, of which 91 percent of the indigenous Timorese were illiterate, and of the remaining 9 percent only a minority had received more than a primary education. This meant that in practice only a tiny proportion of Timorese understood the implications of the choice that was being forced on the country, and those who did were men (women were virtually totally excluded) who had either held positions in government service as civil servants or, though educated, had failed to secure jobs in administration because the Portuguese authorities suspected them of subversive inclinations. This elite for the most part consisted of members of *liurai* and *chefes de suku* families who had the necessary wealth to pay for their children's education. Nevertheless, in May the governor of Portuguese Timor, Fernando Alves Aldeia, issued an official communiqué informing the Timorese they were now at liberty to discuss their political options openly as a prelude for the plebiscite that was promised within twelve months.

Even the educated were inexperienced in politics. During the colonial period the best educated Timorese had never been permitted to engage in political activities beyond, at most, working for a party known as *Acção Nacional Popular.* The "National Action Party," which was neither popular, national, nor a real political party, was a tame creature of the colonial government, and had never taken the lead on anything independent of Lisbon. In April 1974, therefore, ambitious men ignored it and set about fashioning political organizations that would serve as platforms for the alternative visions they held for the future of their country and their own ambitions. Inside a month three political parties had emerged from the ranks of the elite, each organized around one or other of the three options Lisbon had formulated. These organizations were not officially referred to as "parties" because political parties were illegal under the old regime and the new government had not yet repealed the law, so they called themselves "unions," "fronts," or "associations."

The first party to emerge was the *União Democrática Timorense* (UDT) or the Democratic Union of Timor. The leaders of the *União Democrática Timorense* were for the most part men who had adapted successfully to the colonial administration and therefore had held jobs in the bureaucracy. Observers have tended to identify the *União Democrática Timorense* as a party whose platform was to keep Timor subject to Portuguese governance, but as James Dunn (1996) has pointed out, the party, even at the beginning, never discountenanced the option of independence, and its original program called for "progressive autonomy" within a form of Portuguese federation that might permit eventual independence within fifteen or twenty years (Jolliffe 1978:76–77). The second party that came into existence was one originally called the *Associação Social-Democrática Timorense* (ASDT) or the Social Democratic Association of Timor, but in September, a more socialist flavor was imparted to the organization when its name was changed to the *Frente Revolucionária de Timor Leste Independente* or the Revolutionary Front for an Independent East Timor—better known as "Fretilin." The third party was Apodeti, the only party favoring integration into the Republic of

Indonesia. From the time of its creation the party received much less support among the Timorese population, and its leaders were few in number. None the less, as the course of events would prove, it was its platform that—at least in the short run—triumphed.

At the same time it needs to be emphasized that neither the *União Democrática Timorense* nor Fretilin had a monolithic platform. Although from the outset the *União Democrática Timorense* was favored by the more conservative members of the elite class, no one single point of view represented party policy. The views of Domingos de Oliveira and Mário Carrascalão, two of its most influential members, for example, differed little from those of the less socialist-minded members of Fretilin. They also diverged somewhat from the views of their more conservative colleagues, whose connections with the Portuguese administration encouraged them to advocate in no uncertain terms retaining the status quo. Fretilin's range of opinion was expansive enough to embrace those of both José Ramos Horta, whose views, though inclined towards the left, invariably incorporated moderation, and Mário Alkatiri, one of the prime forces in moving the party to the extreme left. The campaign to win over the Timorense increasingly developed a virulent confrontational edge. As if this heterodoxy were not enough, changes in the basic positions of the two parties emerged. The final culmination was reached when the *União Democrática Timorese*, which had never advocated integration with Indonesia, both figuratively and literally went over to the Indonesian side.

The new government—the *Movimento das Forças Armadas* or Armed Forces Movement—that soon replaced the original revolutionaries in Lisbon was rigorously left-wing and did not favor the *União Democrática Timorense* since the latter's platform was considered neo-colonial and its leaders were establishment figures from the all-too-recent discreditable imperial past. Thus, as the Portuguese government intensified its determination to rid itself of Timor, its leaders increasingly came to regard the *União Democrática Timorense* as a serious threat to their plans. Since Fretilin's platform more closely matched that of the *Movimento das Forças Armadas*, Fretilin—from 1974 to September 1975—became the party that the Portuguese government decided to support. The government's bias was demonstrated in its reaction to the experience of Almeida Santos, a lawyer it had commissioned to visit the colony in October 1974 to see how the campaign was progressing. Somewhat to Santos' surprise, it appears, the people of East Timor accorded him an enthusiastic reception. Thousands attended his speeches, and—apart from members and supporters of Fretilin and Apodeti—they showed a firm desire to remain subjects of Portugal. So impressed and taken back was Santos that he assured the Timorese that their wish to remain with Portugal would be respected by the government. When news of his assurances reached Lisbon, however, the Portuguese leaders cautioned him to watch what he said, and moved to intervene by sending to the colony three officials whose mission apparently was to put an end to the relationship between Timor and Portugal as soon as possible. The trio consisted of the new governor of Portuguese Timor, Mário Lemos Pires, Francisco Mota, and Silvério de Costa Jóatas.

By the time they arrived in November 1974 the struggle for power had taken on a distinctive Timorese cast. One feature of Timorese politics is its intensely personal nature. Regardless of political affiliation, almost all the politicians were related, however, distantly, by kinship and marriage, and these ties were reinforced by the social and economic backgrounds the elite had in common. Almost all were domiciled in Dili, the seat of political power in Portuguese Timor, but at the same time they were connected by kinship and marriage with the *liurai* families in the interior rural areas, and it was through the agency of these local chiefs that they were able to exercise influence among the illiterate villagers in the more distant and remote areas of the colony. The intensity of kinship and the small numbers of men who struggled for power elevated the role of personality to a position rare in the upper echelon politics of other countries. Fretilin's president, Francisco Xavier do Amaral, was married to Lucia, a younger sister of an Apodeti leader, José Fernandes Osório Soares. Mário Carrascalão, the most important *União Democrática Timorense* leader, was brother-in-law to José Ramos Horta. Thus feelings that kinship loyalties had been betrayed and disappointments that affinal obligations had been disregarded charged both alliances and hostilities with a special dynamism that often resulted in petty and impulsive reactions to events. These reactions were sufficiently powerful to force the country into an accelerating spiral of violence that was to result in the deaths of tens of thousands of Timorese.

For Timor the aftermath of the April coup in Portugal was the most hectic period in its history up to that time. The Timorese leaders, inexperienced in politics, had to adapt themselves to their new role as well as deal with incompetent politicians in Portugal. Confusion was inevitable, and not only in the interaction between Timorese and Portuguese. Lines of communication between the governor and Lisbon increasingly broke down with the result that when the political campaign began to take on a physically menacing aspect, the government failed to respond. At the most decisive time in its history, when Portuguese Timor was going through more change more rapidly than it ever had in its entire history, the colony was at the mercy of a government that had little time for ensuring that the campaign would be conducted in an orderly manner. For example while the two leading parties were engaged in vituperative exchanges that were to escalate into a civil war that lasted through August and September 1975, Governor Lemos Pires sent more than twenty urgent dispatches to Lisbon, and received a reply to only one (Dunn 1996:83).

On 21 January 1975, the *União Democrática Timorense* and Fretilin formed a coalition, and there were hopes the campaign, in an unexpected move that might have mitigated the deepening tensions, might take on a more conciliatory aspect. On 29 January 1975 Dr. Toby Lazarowitz (1975a), a student of mine who was carrying out fieldwork in Viqueque district at the time, reported in a letter to me that

> many people understand the political problems and the struggle is in many ways a life and death struggle (at least in the eyes of some of the people). Just recently two of the biggest political parties united to form a solid front against the pro-Indonesian Party. This was answered by a statement by the head of the pro-Indonesian group that he was being supported by the Indonesian army. This caused quite as stir as you might have guessed.

But within a matter of weeks when it became apparent Fretilin was winning an increasing number of adherents from *União Democrática Timorense*, influential members of both parties began to reconsider the advisability of the pact.

As the months passed, helped by the crumbling of Portuguese authority, Fretilin tightened its control over the rural areas and gained thousands of new adherents as the *União Democratica Timorense* saw its own support decline. At the same time the Portuguese government began to withdraw its troops from the colony, so that whereas in 1974 there had been around three thousand men, by June 1975 the number was about two hundred. By June in Viqueque Lazarowitz (1975b) was remarking, "The political parties are becoming more polarized and outbreaks of violence are starting to become everyday occurrences" (Lazarowitz 1975b). Suspicions steadily increased between the leaders of the *União Democrática Timorense* and Fretilin, and rumors that one or other party would attempt a coup lent to the months of June and July 1975 an atmosphere of somber expectancy that came to a head on 10–11 August 1975.

On that night *União Democrática Timorense* forces occupied the Comando da Polícia (the police headquarters) in Dili, seized the weapons they discovered, and surrounded the governor's palace and other strategic points in the capital. They took over the main crossroads, the primary radio station, the international communications system, and the airport. Fretilin immediately counterattacked with such success that inside six weeks they had forced the *União Democrática Timorense* army out of Portuguese Timor altogether and over the border into West Timor, where they were welcomed with open arms by the Indonesian army.

The civil war effectively ended on 24 September 1975, and East Timor was now securely in the hands of Fretilin, which seems to have had the backing of most of the population. On 28 November 1975 its leaders declared East Timor independent.

Their lack of experience in democratic politics was a decisive factor in bringing about the civil war, for as I previously noted, none of these "instant politicians" had ever held any sort of political office—or run for any. None had lived in a society where democratic elections were accepted as a matter of course, and as one examines the drama that unfolded on Timor during those turbulent months following the revolution in Lisbon, impressions of political maladroitness are inescapable. Compounding this was the incapacity of the leaders of both sides to find some workable compromise that would have enabled East Timor to establish some kind of viable government acceptable to the government of Indonesia, which was monitoring the course of events very closely indeed. Aversion to compromise tends to be a feature of Timorese political life, and this was part of the reason for the inveterate feuding that characterized rural life in the generations before 1912. In December 1975 internecine fighting again made it possible for an external enemy to conquer the warring parties and take control over their political existence as the Portuguese and Dutch had done centuries before. The enemy on this occasion was the Republic of Indonesia, whose army invaded what now had become known as "East Timor" on 7 December 1975 and began an occupation that was to last until 1999.

The Indonesian administration swiftly moved to impose itself on the country by bringing in administrators, teachers, physicians, and civil engineers, but, above all, an army that for a quarter of a century inflicted harsh measures of control on the Timorese that exceeded in their savagery even that of the Japanese. The total number of Timorese who died will never be known, but the death toll between 1975 and 1999 cannot have been less than 200,000 individuals. Fretilin continued for many years to wage guerilla resistance against the vastly superior Indonesian forces until its most successful leader, José Alexandro Gusmão, was captured and transported to prison in Indonesia.

The international community took no practical measures to prevent the slaughter of Timorese until the atrocities committed against the Timorese by the Indonesian army went too far and brought about a strong reaction from the United States government, which then pressured Indonesia into reconsidering its role in East Timor. The result was that in January 1999 President B. J. Habibie's government agreed to a "Popular Consultation," actually a plebiscite, to take place in the summer by which the Timorese would be given the opportunity to decide, in effect, whether they wished to remain an Indonesian province, which they had been forced to become in July 1976, or become independent.

Even prior to Habibie's proclamation, a curious sociopolitical phenomenon had emerged in the countryside. Gangs of shiftless young men from East Timor, apparently socially rootless, as well as thugs from West

Timor began mobilizing in diverse localities all over the province intimi-dating local people. News about the promised plebiscite transformed these groups into quasi-political entities intent on preventing the Timorese people from casting a vote for independence. Starting in Febru-ary 1999, when threats seemed likely to fail, these gangs—they became known as "militias"—burned down houses, assaulted people, and mur-dered as part of a terrorist campaign to prevent the people of Timor from expressing their wishes in a fair vote. The militias even herded villagers out of their homes and into distant areas where they would not be eligible to register to vote. Anticipating a similar fate, other Timorese fled to the mountains for safety to await patiently the time to register. When it arrived, they descended from the mountains, registered, and prudently returned, to await the day of the election.

Until July the activities of these militias dominated the social and po-litical landscapes, but with the arrival of the United Nations, which had taken responsibility for running the elections, a fitful peace descended on the province, though there were sporadic outbursts of violence until the day of the election. I visited Viqueque town in August 1999 and wit-nessed with my own eyes how inhibiting the presence of the militias was to the local populace. In Mane Hat, shortly before my arrival, a building used by students was burned and people were slain. Then during my visit a militia gang congregated openly in public outside Viqueque town, in a *knua* that was part of the *suku* of Uma Kik, completely unfazed by the In-donesian militia and police force, which took not the slightest interest in the threat they implicitly offered.

The violence remained in check until the day of the referendum, which was on Monday, August 30. I spent that day in two polling stations in the Viqueque region, one at Luca and the other at Dilor. There I wit-nessed the people of East Timor doing something never before permitted them in their history: they were making their wishes known, as a people, in a forum that would actually put those wishes into effect. I watched as thousands of them, many illiterate, left their forested sanctuaries, where they had taken refuge from the militias, for the polling booths. Those who could came on foot. Those too old or infirm hunched themselves up in lit-tle wooden carts pushed by the more able-bodied.

Over the course of the weeks preceding the voting United Nations personnel had laboriously instructed every Timorese they could contact about the procedures of the ballot and the implications of their vote. The U.N. workers were at pains to assure those who had registered that their vote really would be secret, a consideration carrying literal life-and-death implications for them. In the course of events, it was not secrecy that brought about bloodshed but the fact that 78.5 percent of the people who voted had the audacity to choose independence.

The voting was scheduled to begin at 6:30 A.M. in the hundreds of polling centers all over the country. At Dilor thousands of registrants camped outside the polling center during the night, and with the first smear of light in the east they decamped and lined up in front of the six polling booths. Their patience belied their determination. When his or her moment came each person, defying the baneful glares of local militia who were hanging around, entered the makeshift, palm-thatched booths specially constructed for the occasion, and there in isolation offered homage to their vision of a new East Timor. It was a moving sight, the very embodiment of what Westerners take democracy to be, with the literate voters confidently scratching off a "yes" or a "no" with a pencil attached to the wall of the booth by a string, and the illiterates stabbing a nail into a logo representing their choice. But whatever the nature of their media, the message signaled on that day was overwhelming.

Yet there was a heavy price to pay. Reprisals came a few days later when the results were announced, for the militia had not, it appeared, been at all cowed by the hordes of international officials and journalists in the country. The outcome of the plebiscite raised the malevolence of the militia to a level of violence not previously attained. Timorese, United Nations workers, nongovernmental groups, and media correspondents alike were subject to a massive wave of onslaughts. Buildings were razed to the ground, and when I returned two years later there were still thousands of buildings that consisted only of shells of outer walling or blackened skeletons of reinforced concrete. Thousands of Timorese were kidnapped and taken into West Timor, and the foreigners fled the country. Therein lay the seeds of the militia's own destruction, however, for the international community refused to tolerate such a brazen and brutal attack on a process for which the United Nations itself had taken responsibility.

With great reluctance the Indonesian government was obliged—tardily—to accede to the results of the plebiscite, and Australian and United Nations forces went into East Timor to restore order, which they did. The United Nations, now armed with a new mandate to bring about a transition of authority in which the people of East Timor would themselves choose what form of government they wished to have, returned. For over 18 months the United Nations prepared the people of East Timor for yet another vote. This was to determine the composition of an 88-member Constituent Assembly that would create a constitution for the new country, the Democratic Republic of East Timor. Of the 88 members, 75 were to be "at-large" representatives from all over East Timor and the other 13 were to come from each of the 13 districts in the country. On 30 August 2001 the Timorese went to the polls again. No blood was spilt this time, and by December the Constituent Assembly had done its work. Among the provisions formulated by its members was that there would be a president and a prime minister, and who the first incumbents would be was to be determined by an election early the following year. In the event, José Alexandro Gusmão was elected the first president and Mário Alkatiri became the first prime minister of the Democratic Republic of East Timor, which came into existence as an independent nation on Monday, 20 May 2002. Then, on 27 September 2002, the República Democrática de Timor-Leste became the first nation in the twenty-first century to become a member of the United Nations.

Time has taken its toll on Viqueque. Many of my friends from 1966 and 1967 did not survive the maelstrom generated in 1975 by the Indonesian military and revived 24 years later by the militia. In Mamulak in 1999 I attended a party given in honor of a member of the United Nations. There, in Baria Laran, where traditional Tetum houses made of bamboos and palm thatch once stood, was a housing complex of cinder block bungalows parceled out into neat rows. Whereas in the 1960s the Timorese houses were connected by paths that in the dry season rutted so bone-hard you had to take care not to twist your ankle walking on them and in the rainy season were so squelchy your ankles sank into the mud, these were now streets down which you could drive a truck. It hardly needs remarking, therefore, that the Caraubalo of 1966–1967 no longer exists. Many of the local population are dead, not a few at the hands of the Indonesians, but others by more natural processes. André Pereira and Rubi Loik, to name only two of the more prominent personalities described in these pages, are now themselves *mate bein*.

Bad as the occupation was, though, there had been more joyous happenings. On my visit I discovered that André Pereira's son, José, who first introduced me to Mamulak, had married into the most prestigious royal family in all Viqueque—a testimony, indeed, to the respect in which his father was held in the mid-sixties—and I was gratified to learn other persons I had had the pleasure of getting to know are, happily, still contributing to Timorese society, and will doubtless pay prominent roles in the future of their country. Others, still living, with whom I renewed my acquaintance thirty years later made me appreciate even more fully the friendships my wife and I had made during our time in Viqueque.

Appendix

Caraubalo Suku 1966

Village	Total Population	Adult Males	Married Women	Widows	Unmarried Males	Other Females	Language
Cabira Oan	310	105	47	4	60	94	Tetum
Lamaclaran	199	63	31	1	42	62	Tetum
Has Abut	235	72	41	0	61	61	Tetum
Vessa	251	82	41	3	49	76	Tetum
Mane Hat	496	149	80	6	99	162	Tetum
Mamulak	360	116	61	5	72	106	Tetum
Sira Lari	160	47	26	0	44	43	Makassai
	2011	634	327	19	427	604	

Glossary of Selected Tetum Words

ahi matan	Village; clan; hearth.
aiknananoik	Myth; folktale; fable.
aiknananuk	Poem; song.
ai moruk	Medicine.
ali-maun	Clansperson.
alin	Younger sibling.
bahen	Elder; political leader.
banin	Wife's father.
batar	Corn.
buan	Witch.
buran	Betel-chew.
dato	Aristocrat.
dato ua'in	One of the two traditional leaders of Caraubalo *suku*; the other being the *makair fukun*. The office of *dato ua'in* is owned by the Ina Aman clan in the village of Mamulak.
ema banaka	Guests; see *ema mate*.
ema Fehan	The self-designation of the Tetum people in Viqueque.

147

ema Foho	The people who live in the mountains, the Tetum designation for the Makassai.
ema mate	The "people of death"; the kin of a deceased person; see *ema banaka.*
ema moris	The "people who give life," who perform ritual functions when a person in Mamulak or Mane Hat dies.
fe'en	Wife.
ferik	Female elder.
feto	Female; woman; feminine.
feto fuan, mane fuan	"Fruit of the woman, fruit of the man"; lineage.
fetora	Unmarried woman.
fetosá-umane	A form of marriage alliance in which the descent groups exchange the women in an asymmetric manner.
folin	Bridewealth.
fona	Opening; door; vagina.
fukun	See *suku.*
fuluman	Stone altar in the center of a garden.
habani	The second most common form of marriage in Caraubalo. It involves residence for a man with his wife's parents and no bridewealth.
hafoli	The most common form of marriage in Caraubalo. It involves patrilocal residence and bridewealth.
hahoris	To fertilize; to breed; to create; to generate; to beget; to give birth to.
halo batar moris	Corn-planting ritual.
hanek matan mutin	A plate covered with a lid that is used exclusively in rituals.
hare	Rice before it is husked.
hena	A store-bought piece of cloth.
hena mean tahan ida	The sacred cloth; cloth of considerable symbolic value in Tetum ritual. Also called the *hena lolon*, "the womb made of cloth."
inan no aman	Mother and father.
kain	Stalk; stem; descent group; umbilical cord.
karau	Buffalo.
katuas	Married male; elder.
keta mate	Final rite of the death ritual.
klamar	Soul.
klamar mate	Soul of a dead person; a dead soul.
klamar moris	Soul of a living person.

knua	Hamlet.
kohe mate	Pouch of death.
kohe moris	Pouch of life.
kuis	Breath.
la'in	Husband.
lalosan	Virginity.
lawarik mane	Unmarried male; bachelor.
lia tuan	Legend.
lisu	Circular dance.
liurai	King; *suku chief.*
lolon	Container; womb.
lulik	Sacred; prohibited. In Tetum thought and ritual this term is opposed to *sau.*
mahan no leu	People who sit in the shade.
makair fukun	One of the two traditional leaders of Caraubalo *suku*; the other being the *dato ua'in*. The office of *makair fukun* is controlled by the two clans in the village of Mane Hat.
maklaak manu ua'in	Emissaries.
mane	Male; man; masculine.
manu	Cock; bird.
maromak	Masculine divinity that dwells in the sky.
matan	Eye; center; source.
mate	To die; death; dead. Its opposite is *moris.*
mate bein	Ancestral ghost.
maun	Elder brother.
metan	Black.
modok	"The green vegetables"; the five *patacas* and a sacred cloth known as the *hena mean tahan ida*, which forms one of the two parts of the symbolic bridewealth (the *na'an tolu*).
moris	To live; life; to be living. Its opposite is *mate.*
moru ema	"Songs of poison," abusive songs; songs of insult.
na'an	"The meat," of a buffalo, a horse, a pig, and fifty *patacas*, which forms one of the two parts of the symbolic bridewealth (the *na'an tolu*). The other part is called the *modok.*
na'an tolu	That part of the bridewealth that has symbolic significance; the symbolic bridewealth.
nai fei	Grandmother.
nain	Mother.
na'in	Lord.

na'in oan	Grandchild.
oan	Child.
oan feto	Daughter.
oan mane	Son.
pataca	An old Mexican coin imported centuries ago into Timor.
rai	The earth; kingdom; the dwelling place of human beings. This term is opposed in Tetum thought and ritual to *rai laran* or *rai inan*.
rai inan	See *rai laran* and *rai lolon*.
rai laran	The Earth Mother; the dwelling place for ghosts and other spirits; the place where human beings originated and where their bodies and souls return at death.
rai lolon	The womb of the earth. See *rai laran*.
rai na'in	"Lord of the land"; the landlords of Caraubalo *suku*; nature spirits whose domain is the wilderness outside human habitation.
sai oan	Mother's brother's child.
sai rai	"To leave the earth"; the mythological emergence of the first human beings (the earliest inhabitants of Caraubalo) from the earth; the birth ritual that re-enacts this event.
sau; saun	"To lift a prohibition"; "to exempt"; secular; profane; not prohibited. In Tetum thought and ritual this term is opposed to *lulik*.
so'a rai	To till the soil.
suku	Princedom.
tais	Traditional piece of woven cloth, more splendid than *hena*.
tassi feto	Female sea; "northern sea"; Wetar Strait; north.
tassi mane	Male sea; "southern sea"; Timor Sea; south.
ta'uk	Respect; deference; fear.
tei tuak	Grandfather.
tuna	Eel. Also name of a Mamulak clan.
ubu la'in	Great-grandparent.
ubu oan	Great-grandchild.
u'e	Liquid; water; source; a symbolic link between humans and ghosts.
u'e lolo oan	A small water pitcher that is used only in rituals.
u'e matan	Well; spring. Source of life for inhabitants of Caraubalo *suku*, which is a large vent (the "Mahuma vagina") in earth's surface. Used figuratively in various ritual and poetic contexts.

u'e na'in   "Lord of the water"; native spirits whose domain is rivers, streams, and other water sources.

uma   House; building.

References

Barnes, R. H. 1974. *The Kédang: A Study of the Collective Thought of an Eastern Indonesian People.* Oxford: Clarendon Press.

Bloch, Maurice. 1971. *Placing the Dead: Tombs, Ancestral Villages, and Kinship Organization in Madagascar.* London and New York: Seminar Press.

Bloch, Maurice, and Jonathan Parry. 1982. Introduction. In *Death and the Regeneration of Life*, edited by Maurice Bloch and Jonathan Parry, 1–44. Cambridge: Cambridge University Press.

Boxer, Charles. 1960. Portuguese Timor: A Rough Island History. *History* 10: 349–55.

Brandewie, Ernest and Simon Asten. 1976. Northern Belunese (Tetum) Marriage and Kinship: A Study of Symbols. *Philippine Quarterly of Culture and Society* 4: 19–30.

Cinatti, Rui. 1987. *Motivos Artísticos Timorenses e a Sua Integração.* Lisbon: Instituto de Investigação Científico Tropical Museu de Etnologia.

Coates, Brian J., and Dana Gardner. 1997. *A Guide to the Birds of Wallacea.* Alderly, Queensland, Australia: Dove Publications Pty. Ltd.

Coèdes, Georges. 1968. *The Indianized States of Southeast Asia*, 3rd. ed. Honolulu: East-West Center.

Cortesão, Armando. (ed.). 1944. *The Suma Oriental of Tomé Pires.* London: Hakluyt Society, Series 2:89.

Costa, Luís. 2000. *Dicionário de Tetum-Português.* Lisbon: Edições Colibri, Faculdade de Letras da Universidade de Lisboa.

Delaney, Carol. 1991. *The Seed and the Soil: Gender and Cosmology in Turkish Village Society.* Berkeley: University of California Press.

Dores, Raphael das. 1907. *Diccionário Teto-Português.* Lisbon: Imprensa Nacional.

Duarte, Jorge Barros. 1979. Barlaque: Casamento Gentílico Timorense. *Arquivos do Centro Cultural Português, Fundação Calouste Gulbenkian, Paris* 14: 377–418.

Dunn, James. 1996. *Timor: A People Betrayed*, 2d ed. Sydney: ABC Books for the Australian Broadcasting Corporation.

Durkheim, Émile. 1960. *Les structures élémentaires de la vie religieuse: le système totémique en Australie*, 4th ed. Paris: Bibliothèque de Philosophie Contemporaine Fondée par Félix Alcan, Press Universitaires de France.

Evans-Pritchard, E. E. 1951. *Social Anthropology.* London: Cohen & West.

Felgas, Helio A. Esteves. 1956. *Timor Português.* Lisbon: Agencie Geral do Ultramar.

Forth, Gregory. 1981. *Rindi: An Ethnographic Study of a Traditional Domain in Eastern Sumba.* The Hague: Martinus Nijhoff.

———. 1992. The Pigeon and the Friarbird: The Mythical Origin of Death and Daylight in East Indonesia. *Anthropos* 87: 423–41.

———. 1998. *Beneath the Volcano: Religion, Cosmology and Spirit Classification among the Nage of Eastern Indonesia.* Leiden: Koninklijk Instituut voor Taal- en Volkenkunde Press.

Foster, Mary Le Cron. 1979. Synthesis and Antithesis in Balinese Ritual. In *The Imagination of Reality: Essays in Southeast Asian Coherence Systems,* edited by A. L. Becker and Aram A. Yengoyan, 175–96. Norwood, NJ: Ablex Publishing Corporation.

Francillon, Gérard. 1967. Some Matriarchic Aspects of the Social Structure of the Southern Tetun of Middle Timor. Ph. D. Diss., Canberra, The Australian National University.

Grijzen, H. J. 1904. Mededeelingen omtrent Beloe of Midden-Timor. *Verhandelingen van het Bataviaasch Genootschap van Kunsten en Wetenschappen* 54.

Hertz, Robert. 1907. Contribution à une étude sur la représentation collective de la mort. *Année Sociologique* 10: 48–137.

Hicks, David. 1984. *A Maternal Religion: The Role of Women in Tetum Myth and Ritual.* DeKalb: Northern Illinois University Center for Southeast Asian Studies.

———. 1988. Literary Masks and Metaphysical Truths. *American Anthropologist* 90: 807–17.

———. 1990. *Kinship and Religion in Eastern Indonesia.* Gothenburg Studies in Social Anthropology, vol. 12. Gothenburg: Acta Universitatis Gothoburgensis.

———. 1996. Making the King Divine: A Case Study in Ritual Regicide from Timor. *Journal of the Royal Anthropological Institute (N.S.)* 2: 611–24.

———. 1997. Friarbird on Timor: Two Mambai Narratives of Avian Rivalry. *Anthropos* 92: 198–200.

Hocart, A. M. 1954. *Social Origins.* London: Watts and Co.

———. 1970 [1936]. *Kings and Councillors: An Essay in the Comparative Anatomy of Human Society.* Edited by Rodney Needham. Chicago and London: The University of Chicago Press.

Hull, Geoffrey. 1999. *Standard Tetum-English Dictionary.* St. Leonards, New South Wales, Australia: Allen & Unwin in association with the University of Western Sydney Macarthur.

Jolliffe, Jill. 1978. *East Timor: Nationalism and Colonialism.* Brisbane: University of Queensland Press.

Lazarowitz, Toby Fred. 1975a. Unpublished Letter dated January 29.

———. 1975b. Unpublished Letter dated June 21.

Leal, Ondina Fachel. 1994. The Gaucho Cockfight in Porto Alegre, Brazil. In *The Cockfight: A Casebook,* edited by Alan Dundes, 208–31. Madison: University of Wisconsin Press.

Lukes, Steven. 1985. *Emile Durkheim: His Life and Work,* 2d ed. Stanford: Stanford University Press.

Matos, Artur Teodoro de. 1974. *Timor Português 1515–1769: Contribuçâo para a sua História*. Lisbon: Faculdade de Letras da Universidade de Lisboa Instituto Histórico Infante Dom Henrique.

Metzner, Joachim. 1977. *Man and Environment in Eastern Timor*. Development Studies Center, Monograph 8. Canberra: The Australian National University.

Molnar, Andrea Katalin. 2000. *Grandchildren of the Ga'e Ancestors: Social Oganization and Cosmology Among the Hoga Sara of Flores*. Leiden: Koninklijk Instituut voor Taal- en Volkenkunde Press.

Morris, Cliff. 1984. *Tetun-English Dictionary*. Canberra: The Australian National University.

Muir, Edward. 1997. *Ritual in Early Modern Europe*. Cambridge: Cambridge University Press.

Needham, Rodney. 1978. *Primordial Characters*. Charlottesville: University Press of Virginia.

Pascoal, E. 1949. O Culto dos "Lulic." *Seara* 1, no. 1, January: 12–15.

Sá, Artur Basílio de. 1961. *Textos em Teto Literatura Oral Timorense*. Lisbon: Junta de Investigações.

Schulte Nordholt, H. G. 1971. *The Political System of the Atoni of Timor*. Translated by M. J. L. van Yperen. Verhandelingen Van Het Koninklijk Instituut Voor Taal-, Land- en Volkenkunde 60. The Hague: Martinus Nijhoff.

Silva, Ramos da. n.d. *Dicionário Tetum-Português*.

Smith, William Robertson. 1956 (1889). *The Religion of the Semites*. New York: Meridian.

Therik, Gerzon Tom. 1995. Wehali: The Four Corner Land: The Cosmology and Traditions of a Timorese Ritual Center. Ph. D. Diss., Canberra, Australia, The Australian National University.

Thomaz, Luís Filipe F.R. 1977. *Timor: autopsia de uma tragedia*. Lisbon: Author, distributed by Dig/livro.

Valeri, Valerio. 1990. Both Nature and Culture: Reflections on Menstrual and Parturitional Taboos in Huaulu (Seram). In *Power and Difference: Gender in Island Southeast Asia*, edited by Jane Atkinson and Shirley Errington, 235–72. Stanford: Stanford University Press.

Vondra, J. Gert. 1968. *Timor Journey*. Wellington/Auckland, New Zealand: A. H. and A. W. Reed.

Vroklage, B. A. G. 1952–1953. *Ethnographie der Belu in Zentral-Timor*, 3 volumes. Leiden: E. J. Brill.

Wolters, O. W. 1967. *Early Indonesian Commerce*. Ithaca: Cornell University Press.

Wortelboer, Wilco von. 1955. Zur Sprache und Kultur der Belu (Timor). *Anthropos* 50: 155–200.

Index